500

barbecue dishes

500
barbecue dishes

the only barbecue compendium you'll ever need

Paul Kirk

SELLERS
PUBLISHING

A Quintet Book

Published by Sellers Publishing, Inc.
161 John Roberts Road, South Portland, Maine 04106

For ordering information:
(800) 625-3386 Toll Free
(207) 772 6814 Fax

Visit our Web site: www.rsvp.com • E-mail: rsp@rsvp.com

ISBN: 978-1-4162-0509-8
e-ISBN: 978-1-4162-0824-2
QTT.BQS

This book was conceived, designed, and produced by
Quintet Publishing Limited
6 Blundell Street
London N7 9BH
United Kingdom

Library of Congress Control Number: 2007936994

Managing Editor: Donna Gregory
Editorial Assistant: Robert Davies
Designer: Dean Martin
Art Director: Sofia Henry
Photography: Ian Garlick
Food Stylist: Judith Fertig
Publisher: Gillian Laskier

10 9 8 7 6 5 4 3

Manufactured in Singapore by Pica Digital Pte Ltd.
Printed in China by 1010 Printing International Ltd.

Cover photograph © jupiterimages

contents

introduction   6

sizzling appetizers   14

flaming fish and shellfish   46

chargrilled chicken and poultry   80

perfect pork and lamb   114

succulent beef   152

vegetarian bites   198

salads and sides   230

sweet sizzlers   258

index   282

getting fired up

"Grilling" means cooking food directly over a heat source, sealing the food on the outside with a beautifully charred crust while the inside remains tender and juicy. Strictly speaking, "barbecuing" refers to cooking over indirect heat, under a cover, allowing heat to be conducted around the food as in an oven. Nowadays people use the terms "grilling" and "barbecuing" interchangeably, and this book goes along with the trend, taking care to specify when the indirect, covered method of cooking is intended.

choosing your barbecue grill

Choosing a grill can be a difficult decision as so many cooking vessels are included under that term, from a hole in the ground to an elaborate structure that serves effectively as an outdoor kitchen. The most widely available options are explained below so that you can choose wisely.

Charcoal grills are said by purists to be the only option. They claim that charcoal is the only way to achieve a genuine smoky flavor in the grilled food; and they believe the act of stoking and tending a fire to be basic to the age-old experience of outdoor grilling. Operating a charcoal grill, though, requires more skill than electric or gas versions.

Gas grills are easier to control than charcoal grills and can be made ready for use almost immediately. The lava rocks or flavoring plates that cook the food are heated by propane or natural gas. They are an excellent choice for a grill that is going to be used frequently.

Electric grills are available in small portable forms or as large trolley grills. They provide a good constant heat source but cannot reach the high temperatures of charcoal. They must be used close to a power source or with a long extension cord.

the right fuel for charcoal grills

Natural charcoal burns hotter and cleaner than artificial charcoal briquettes. It ignites quickly and burns well for about 45 minutes, perfect for searing food quickly.

Briquette charcoal is made from compressed charcoal particles that are impregnated with chemicals to help it ignite more easily. It burns for longer than natural charcoal and provides a steady heat source.

Wood can be used in the form of logs, chunks, or chips. Don't use resinous soft woods such as pine. A handful of wood chips thrown onto hot coals will impart different flavors to your grill — try cherry wood for a slightly sweet smoke; mesquite for strong, earthy flavors; or hickory for a pungently smoky flavor.

lighting up

Your grill should be sited on solid, level ground away from low trees. Clean and oil it before use, and always preheat it so that it reaches the desired temperature before you begin to cook. When lighting up, make sure you are dressed sensibly in heatproof mitts and a protective apron, and keep children and animals away. Never light up in a high wind and be sure to keep matches and lighter fuels a safe distance away from the flame. In the event of a flare-up, use your spritzer bottle of water or a handful of baking soda to douse the flames.

maintaining your grill

Each time you are preparing to grill, check that the connecting hoses and taps are in good order on a gas grill. Periodically check the wires and circuits on an electric grill. Oil your grill racks regularly — ideally every time you are preparing to light it — so that food does not stick. Keep the grill grease-free by scrubbing with a wire brush after cooking. When the ashes have cooled, clean them from your firebox and dispose of them in a lidded trash can.

best cuts for the grill

poultry and game

Whole birds and juicy cuts—such as thighs and wings—are the best choices. A large, whole bird will not cook on an open grill unless it is split or cut into joints. However, it can be spit-roasted if you have this facility. Always pierce the bird between the thigh and breast—when the liquid runs clear the bird is cooked. Split a bird by placing it on its back and cutting through either side of the backbone, removing it completely. Turn the bird over and flatten with the heel of your hand. Jointing will provide two breasts, thighs, drumsticks, and wings.

lamb

Loin and sirloin chops, steaks from the leg, and fillets are all good cuts for grilling. To prepare chops, trim all but a thin layer of fat from the outside and any other excess fat. This will help minimize flare-ups. Kabobs are best made from a shoulder joint. Meat from the leg is leaner. Ground lamb can be made from shoulder or cheaper cuts. Put the meat through the mincer two or three times at least to ensure a smooth paste.

pork

Pork tends to be a little tougher than beef or lamb. Because it needs to be well cooked, there is a danger that it may dry out; it will therefore benefit greatly from being marinated. Spareribs, chops, and tenderloin are all suitable for grilling, as is ground pork. To prepare, trim all but a $\frac{1}{2}$-inch of layer fat from the outside of chops, and any other visible excess fat. Spareribs benefit from long, slow cooking, and may be precooked in an oven, leaving the last 15 minutes of grilling to be carried out on an open charcoal fire.

beef

Choose the best quality meat that you can afford. Rump, sirloin, fillet, T-bone, porterhouse, and rib steak are the most tender cuts and best able to withstand high heat without becoming tough. Look for lean meat with a fine marbling of fat, which will keep the meat moist during cooking. To prepare beef, trim the border fat to a thickness of $1/2$ inch. This will minimize flare-ups but leave sufficient fat to keep the meat moist. With the point of a sharp knife, cut through the sinew and remaining fat around the edge at 1-inch intervals to avoid curling during cooking.

fish

The range of fish and shellfish available for grilling is enormous. Whether the fish is large or small, whole or filleted, it will cook to a delicate and delicious flakiness. Oily fish such as salmon and mackerel are an excellent choice. To keep the fish moist, marinate it first and brush it frequently with oil during cooking. Fish can also be wrapped in vine leaves, lettuce, or bacon to help prevent it from drying out. It can also be cooked in heavy-duty weight aluminum foil packages, although it will lose the smoky flavor done this way. If you are making kabobs, use only firm fish such as monkfish or salmon.

temperatures

Cooking times depend on the heat of the grill and the thickness of the food being cooked. As a rough guide to temperature, the fire is hot if you can only bear to hold your hand 6 inches above the grill for just two seconds. This is suitable for searing. The fire is medium-hot if you can hold your hand over the heat at the same height for four seconds, and low if you can hold your hand there for more than six seconds.

approximate cooking times

6-oz. boneless chicken breast	7 to 8 minutes on each side
6-oz. boneless chicken thigh	4 to 5 minutes on each side
8-oz. chicken drumstick	15 to 20 minutes, turning often
9-oz. chicken quarter	25 to 30 minutes, turning often
1-lb. 11-oz. chicken half	35 to 40 minutes, turning often
Chicken wing	20 to 25 minutes, turning often
Chicken liver	15 to 20 minutes, turning often
Boneless duck breast	10 minutes on each side
Turkey breast	10 to 12 minutes on each side
7- to 9-oz. fish steak, about 1-in. thick	4 to 5 minutes on each side
Small fish, up to 10 oz.	6 to 7 minutes on each side
3-lb. 6-oz. whole fish	12 to 15 minutes on each side
Kabob, 1-in. cubes of fish	7 to 8 minutes on each side
Large shrimp, unshelled	2 to 3 minutes on each side
Zucchini or eggplant, 3/4-in. thick slices	6 to 8 minutes, turning once
Potato or sweet potato, 5-oz. pieces	30 minutes, turning once
Tomato, halved	10 to 15 minutes
Mushroom cap	4 minutes
Onion, whole	45 to 50 minutes
1-in. thick lamb chop	8 to 10 minutes on each side
6-oz lamb fillet	4 to 5 minutes on each side
1 1/2-in. thick lamb leg steak	6 to 7 minutes on each side
Lamb or pork kabob	10 to 15 minutes, turning often
1-in. thick pork chop	8 to 10 minutes on each side
1-lb. pork tenderloin	25 minutes, turning often

Single pork ribs	1 hour, turning often
1-inch thick rump or sirloin steak, medium well done	5 to 6 minutes on each side
1 1/2-inch thick fillet steak, medium well done	7 to 8 minutes on each side
1-inch thick burger, medium well done	5 minutes on each side

smoking

Smoking is a way of preparing meat or fish by exposing it to the aromatic smoke of burning hardwood after it has been salted or pickled for a time in brine. Traditionally this method was used to keep food edible for long periods; nowadays it is principally used to add flavor. Home smoking is easy: you can make a smoker out of any barbecue grill or pit which has a cover, so long as the temperature is controllable. You must be able to adjust the airflow to the heat source, which will control the heat of the fire (with less oxygen the fire will burn more slowly), and you need to be able to regulate the escaping air as this affects how much smoke will be kept in the food chamber. Hardwood is the classic smoldering agent and you could experiment widely with different types of wood and the scents of their smoke.

setting up your smoker

You need wood chips or chunks for flavor as well as charcoal for heat. I also suggest you use a water pan, which will keep the atmosphere in the smoker humid and help retain moisture in the food. Place your hot coals over an air vent if possible; this will allow you to control the heat by allowing air into and out of the smoker. Place the water pan right up against the hot coals. Place the meat on the smoker and place the lid on top, with the vent holes opposite the hot coals. Cook until ready. If you are smoking for more than about an hour, replenish the coals with hot ones as needed.

marinades and rubs

The basic items in any barbecue cook's repertoire are the seasonings that can be applied to a joint of meat, piece of fish, or array of vegetables a few hours in advance, allowing their flavors to soak into the food.

garlic-herb butter
Try this melted over simply grilled fish or asparagus.

2 sticks butter, softened
1/4 cup canola oil
1/4 cup buttermilk
1 tbsp. torn fresh basil leaves

1 tbsp. fresh oregano leaves
12 cloves garlic, pressed
1 tsp. sea salt
1/8 tsp. cayenne pepper

Combine all of the ingredients and blend well. Form into logs and wrap in plastic wrap. Chill in a refrigerator and slice as needed. Vary the taste by adding 2 cups grated cheddar cheese to make a garlic-cheese butter, or roasting the garlic for 45 minutes in a hot oven before peeling the cloves and mashing them into the butter.

basic barbecue rub
Rub this into steaks or chops before cooking for a classic barbecue flavor.

1/4 cup granulated sugar
1 tbsp. seasoned salt
1 tbsp. garlic salt
1 tbsp. onion salt
1 tbsp. celery salt
2 tbsp. sweet paprika

1 tbsp. chili powder
1 tbsp. ground black pepper
1/2 tsp. ground ginger
1/2 tsp. ground allspice
1/2 tsp. dry mustard
1/4 tsp. cayenne pepper

Stir all the ingredients together and blend well. Store in an airtight container in a cool, dark place. You can create your own barbecue rubs using this formula, making sure to get a balance between sugar and salt, always to use paprika for color, and to add up to a teaspoon of each of your three favorite seasonings. If you want heat, add up to a teaspoon of the chili-based seasoning you prefer.

tomato barbecue sauce

Barbecue sauces need a base — tomato, vinegar, or mustard — as well as both a sweet and sour element, and the spices and seasonings of your choice. This one is a winner. Throughout this book, where recipes call simply for "barbecue sauce," use either the recipe below or a good store-bought version.

2 cups ketchup	1 tsp. fine grind black pepper
1/2 cup dark brown sugar	2 tsp. salt
1/4 cup white wine vinegar	1 tsp. ground allspice
2 tbsp. Worcestershire sauce	1 tsp. garlic powder
1 tsp. liquid smoke	1 tsp. dry mustard
1 tbsp. chili powder	1/4 tsp. chipotle powder

Combine all the dry ingredients in a saucepan. Add the liquid ingredients, except the ketchup. Stir well until all are incorporated. Stir in the ketchup and blend in. Bring the mixture slowly to a boil, reduce the heat, and simmer gently for 20 minutes, stirring occasionally. (Be careful when boiling ketchup as it pops and spits.) Let cool. Store in the refrigerator before use.

sizzling appetizers

Barbecues are perfect for bite-size appetizers, ideal for getting the mouth watering before the main event! Prepare some enticing treats on the grill to offer when your guests arrive — perhaps some grilled quesadillas or buffalo wings with hot pepper sauce, grilled oysters, or skewered shrimp with sweet chili sauce.

stuffed monterey mushrooms

see variations page 34

Tasty stuffed mushrooms are always a favorite party appetizer. This recipe is perfect for any occasion.

24 medium mushrooms
1 lb. spiced sausage
8 oz. cream cheese

1/2 cup Monterey Jack cheese, grated
1 tbsp. crushed red pepper flakes
2 tbsp. grated Parmesan cheese

Wash the mushrooms, remove the stems, and pat the caps dry with paper towels. Preheat the grill to 250°F (120°C).

Cook the sausage in a large skillet until done, drain, and place in a mixing bowl. Add the cream cheese, Monterey Jack cheese, and crushed red pepper flakes. Mix well. Place 1 heaped teaspoon of the mixture into each mushroom cap. Place the stuffed mushroom caps on a baking pan with a lip that will fit into your grill, sprinkle with Parmesan, and smoke-roast, covered, for 30 to 45 minutes. Remove and let cool for 5 minutes. Arrange the stuffed mushrooms on a decorative serving platter.

Serves 8

barbecued wings

see variations page 35

Sticky barbecued chicken wings are a perennial favorite and a great snack to offer before the main event. You can't make too many — they will disappear as fast as you can make them!

2 tsp. coarse sea salt or kosher salt
1 tsp. freshly ground black pepper
1 tsp. paprika
1 tsp. chili powder

1/2 tsp. ground celery seeds
3 lbs. wings, tips removed
    and dejointed
1 1/2 cups barbecue sauce

Combine the salt, pepper, paprika, chili powder, and celery seeds. Blend well. Roll the wings in this mixture. Grill over medium heat directly or with indirect heat, covered. Turn the wings about every 10 minutes for 30 minutes to 1 hour, depending on how hot you are cooking.

When the wings are done, place in a large stainless steel bowl and pour the sauce over them. Toss to coat with the sauce. Serve hot.

Serves 6–8

charcoal-grilled skewered shrimp

see variations page 36

Quickly grilled shrimp retain their natural sweetness and sea-fresh flavor.

2 lbs. large shrimp in the shell
   (20–25 count)
1/3 cup canola oil
1/2 cup fresh lime juice
3 tbsp. dry white wine or vermouth
1 clove garlic, pressed

1 tbsp. minced shallots or green onions
   (white part only)
1 tsp. sea salt
1 1/2 tsp. minced fresh dill or 1/2 tsp. dried
Several dashes Louisiana hot sauce

Place the shrimp in a shallow ceramic or glass baking dish. Combine the remaining ingredients and pour over the shrimp. Cover and chill for several hours or overnight. Drain the shrimp and reserve the marinade.

Thread the shrimp on skewers or place in a wire grill basket. Grill the shrimp over hot coals, turning and brushing with the reserved marinade, until pink and cooked through, about 4 to 5 minutes. Serve with wooden toothpicks.

Makes 30 servings

grilled oysters san felipe

see variations page 37

This spicy sauce is the perfect foil for fresh oysters cooked in the half-shell.

20 oysters in shells
for the sauce
2 tbsp. finely minced onion
1 tbsp. unsalted butter
2 tbsp. all-purpose flour
4 oz. bottled clam juice
4 oz. flat beer
2 tsp. Tabasco

2 tbsp. freshly grated Parmesan cheese
for the crumb topping
1/4 cup fine dry Italian breadcrumbs
1/4 cup freshly grated Parmesan cheese
2 tbsp. unsalted butter, melted
1 tbsp. chopped cilantro
1 tsp. Tabasco

Clean, open, and shuck oysters. Place oysters in their rinsed and dried bottom shell halves. In a small saucepan cook the onion in 1 tablespoon butter until soft. Stir in flour; add clam juice, beer, and Tabasco. Cook and stir until thickened and bubbly. Remove from heat and stir in 2 tablespoons Parmesan cheese.

Combine bread crumbs, 1/4 cup cheese, 2 tablespoons melted butter, cilantro, and 1 teaspoon Tabasco. Spoon a scant tablespoon of sauce over each oyster; sprinkle 1 teaspoon of crumb mixture on top. Line a shallow pan with rock salt to a depth of 1/2 inch (or use crumpled foil to prevent shells from tipping), creating dips to cradle the shell halves. Grill over medium heat for 8 to 10 minutes or until heated through.

Serves 10

bacon wraps

see variations page 38

The soft meatiness of these simple wraps is lifted by the crunch of the water chestnut.

One 8-oz. can water chestnuts, drained
1 lb. thinly sliced bacon, cut in half
1 cup chicken livers, cut in pieces

Water-soaked toothpicks
1/4 cup soy sauce
1/2 cup loosely packed light brown sugar

Place a water chestnut on a bacon slice and top with a piece of chicken liver. Wrap the bacon over the top of the liver and secure with a toothpick. (Roll or screw in the toothpick to reduce broken water chestnuts.)

Repeat until you fill a casserole dish (one layer only). Mix the soy sauce and brown sugar, and sprinkle over the top of the appetizers.

Grill over medium heat, covered, turning occasionally. Cook for about 0 to 10 minutes, or until bacon is crisp and browned. Serve with cocktail picks.

Serves 8

bbq sweet and spicy meatballs

see variations page 39

These richly flavored meatballs make a tempting informal appetizer. If you're handing them out with drinks, serve them with toothpicks. If you're serving them at the table, serve chunks of bread for mopping up the luscious sauce.

1 1/2 lbs. ground chuck
1 cup breadcrumbs
1/2 cup milk
1 large egg, lightly beaten
1 tbsp. Worcestershire sauce
1/4 cup grated Parmesan cheese
2 tsp. kosher salt
1 tsp. freshly ground black pepper

1 tbsp. garlic powder
1 tbsp. onion powder
2 tsp. dried oregano
2 tsp. dried basil
for the sauce
2 cups barbecue sauce or favorite salsa
1 cup seedless raspberry jam
1 tsp. chipotle powder

Preheat your smoker or grill to between 230°F and 250°F (110°C and 120°C). Line a sheet pan with foil for easy cleanup. Set aside. Combine ground chuck, breadcrumbs, milk, egg, Worcestershire sauce, cheese, salt, pepper, garlic, onion powder, oregano, and basil. Form into 1-inch meatballs and place on lined sheet pan so they are not touching each other. Barbecue for 45 minutes to 1 hour or until cooked through.

While meatballs are grilling, bring the barbecue sauce, raspberry jam, and chipotle powder to a simmer, stirring until well combined. Toss cooked meatballs with raspberry sauce until well coated. Serve in a chafing dish or slow cooker to keep warm.

Makes approximately 50 meatballs

grilled pizza

see variations page 40

You can use pita bread or tortillas for the pizza crust instead of this straightforward homemade bread dough.

1 1/2 tsp. dried yeast
1 cup lukewarm water
1/2 tsp. sugar
3 cups all-purpose flour
3 tbsp. olive oil

1/4 cup tomato sauce
6 oz. sliced pepperoni
1 red bell pepper, roasted, skinned, and sliced
3/4 cup pitted and sliced black olives
8 oz. mozzarella cheese

Combine yeast, water, and sugar together and let stand in a warm place until the mixture starts to foam. Add the yeast mixture to the flour and oil, and combine to form a dough. Knead on a lightly floured surface until smooth and elastic.

Cover and stand in a warm place until doubled in size. Meanwhile, lightly oil a baking sheet. Punch down the dough and roll out to a rectangle the size of the baking sheet, and place onto the sheet.

Spread the dough with tomato sauce and top with pepperoni, red peppers, olives, and cheese. Cook the pizza indirectly on high heat, covered, for approximately 20 minutes. Place baking sheet directly over one burner on high for approximately 2 minutes to crisp the base.

Serves 6–8

grilled quesadillas

see variations page 41

This Mexican staple is ideal served with salsa, guacamole, or a black-bean dip.

4 flour tortillas (10-in. diameter)   Freshly ground pepper
1 cup shredded Monterey Jack cheese

Prepare a charcoal fire or preheat a gas grill for direct grilling over medium heat.

Lay the tortillas on a flat work surface. Sprinkle half of each tortilla with 1/4 cup cheese
and some pepper. You can add other fillings if you like; divide them among the tortillas,
distributing them evenly over the cheese. Fold the empty half of the tortilla over the filled
portion.

The tortillas are not sealed, so you need to be careful when you transfer them to the
grill — use a wide burger flipper to do so. Grill for about 6 minutes in total, turning
over once (carefully) halfway through the cooking time. Cut each quesadilla into
4 wedges before serving.

Serves 4

tomato-basil bruschetta

see variations page 42

A popular Italian classic, this is both simple to prepare and a joy to eat!

4 or 5 medium, ripe tomatoes, peeled and
  coarsely chopped
1/3 cup olive oil
3 tbsp. balsamic vinegar
1/8 cup chopped fresh basil or 1/2 tsp. dried

Pinch of freshly ground black pepper
1 long baguette or 1 loaf Italian bread, cut into
  1/2-in. slices
4 cloves garlic, sliced in half
Freshly grated Parmesan cheese, if desired

Drain tomatoes in a strainer for 20 minutes. Combine oil, vinegar, basil, and pepper in a large bowl and whisk together. Add drained tomatoes to the dressing and toss to coat. Allow to marinate for at least 15 minutes, or up to 30 minutes.

Toast bread slices on both sides on a medium-hot grill. When toasted, rub the cut side of the garlic on the top of each slice. Top each slice with some of the tomato mixture. You may serve this now or, if desired, sprinkle with Parmesan cheese and return to the grill, covered, until it melts. (It doesn't take long.)

Makes 10–12 slices

thai chicken satay skewers

see variations page 43

Creamy peanut sauce with tender skewered chicken is a deservedly popular Thai classic.

1 lb. boneless, skinless chicken breasts
for the marinade
1/3 cup soy sauce
2 tbsp. fresh lime juice
2 cloves garlic, pressed
2 tsp. grated fresh gingerroot
1 tsp. crushed red pepper flakes

2 tbsp. water
for the peanut sauce
3/4 cup canned unsweetened coconut milk
1 tbsp. creamy peanut butter
4 green onions with tops cut into 1-in. pieces
36 water-soaked bamboo skewers

Cut the chicken into 1/4-inch-wide strips; place in a shallow dish. Combine the soy sauce, lime juice, garlic, ginger, and red pepper flakes in a bowl. Set aside 3 tablespoons of the mixture; cover and refrigerate. Add water to the remaining mixture. Pour over the chicken and toss to coat. Cover the chicken and marinate in refrigerator for between 30 minutes and 2 hours, stirring occasionally.

Preheat a grill to medium. Meanwhile, combine coconut milk, the 3 tablespoons reserved marinade, and peanut butter in small saucepan. Bring to a boil over medium-high heat, stirring constantly. Reduce heat and simmer 2 to 4 minutes, until the sauce thickens. Keep warm. Drain the chicken and discard the marinade. Weave 3 to 4 chicken strips accordion-style onto each skewer, alternating with green onion pieces. Grill the skewers on the uncovered grill for 6 to 8 minutes or until the chicken is cooked. Turn halfway through grilling time. Serve with warm peanut sauce for dipping.

Makes 36 skewers

marinated grilled artichokes

see variations page 44

Grilling artichokes is the perfect way to prepare them, as they maintain a firm texture.
Their unique flavor is enhanced by the simple marinade.

4 large artichokes
1/4 cup balsamic vinegar
1/4 cup water

1/4 cup soy sauce
1 tbsp. grated fresh gingerroot
1/4 cup olive oil

Trim the stems off the artichokes, leaving about 2 inches of stem on each artichoke. Cut off
the shar point on each leaf. Boil or steam artichokes until bases pierce easily, or a leaf pulls
off easily. Drain artichokes and cool. Cut each artichoke in half lengthwise and scrape out
fuzzy center and any purple-tipped leaves.

Mix remaining ingredients in a large plastic bag. Place artichokes in the bag and coat all
sides of the artichokes. Marinate for at least 1 hour, but for best flavor marinate in the
mixture overnight in the refrigerator

Drain artichokes, reserving marinade. Place cut side down on a grate over medium heat. Grill
until lightly browned on the cut side, 5 to 7 minutes. Turn artichokes over and drizzle some
of the remaining marinade over them. Grill until leaf tips are lightly charred, 3 to 4 minutes
more. Serve hot or at room temperature.

Makes 8 servings

bacon-wrapped jalapeño poppers

see variations page 45

These Southern favorites are easy to prepare in advance, as you can chill or freeze them before frying. Increase the quantities to suit; you can never have too many!

25 fresh jalapeño peppers	Two 16-oz. packages bacon
14-16 oz. cream cheese, softened	1/4 cup dark brown sugar
2 cups grated cheddar cheese	Water-soaked toothpicks

Use hot or mild jalapeño peppers, according to your preference. Cut the tops off the jalapeños. Remove the veins and seeds.

Combine the cheeses and blend until they are soft enough to pipe through a pastry bag. Fill the jalapeños. Slice the bacon strips in half and coat with the dark brown sugar. Wrap the bacon around the jalapeños, covering the opened end, and secure with a toothpick.

Stand the peppers upright together in an aluminum pan so the cheese won't come out. Get your smoker up to 230°F–250°F (110°C–120°C) and smoke the poppers for about 1 hour, or until bacon is done.

Makes 25

variations

stuffed monterey mushrooms

see base recipe page 15

crab-stuffed mushrooms
Replace stuffing with a crabmeat stuffing. Sauté 1 tablespoon butter, 2 pressed cloves garlic, 4 sliced green onions, 6 ounces drained and flaked crab meat, and 1 cup fresh breadcrumbs. Cool and add 5 ounces minced water chestnuts, 1/2 cup mayonnaise, and salt and pepper to taste.

blue cheese-stuffed mushrooms
Replace stuffing with this mixture: sauté 8 oz. crumbled blue cheese; 2 pressed cloves garlic; 10 oz. frozen chopped spinach, thawed and drained; 2 ounces unsalted butter at room temperature; salt and pepper to taste. Cool before handling.

bacon and olive-stuffed mushrooms
Replace stuffing with a mixture of 3/4 cup grated Parmesan cheese, 1/2 cup minced olives, 2 tablespoons Worcestershire sauce, and 14 bacon slices that have been cooked crisp and crumbled.

roasted red pepper-stuffed mushrooms
Replace stuffing with a mixture of 8 ounces softened cream cheese, 2 ounces roasted red pepper, 2 tablespoons grated Parmesan cheese, 2 pressed cloves garlic, and 1/2 teaspoon chipotle powder.

barbecued wings

see base recipe page 16

grilled buffalo wings
Replace barbecue sauce with buffalo sauce. Combine 1/4 cup Louisiana hot sauce,
4 tablespoons margarine, 1 tablespoon Worcestershire sauce, and 1 teaspoon lemon juice.

barbecued tex-mex wings
Omit the celery seeds in the seasoning mix. Replace barbecue sauce with a spicy Tex-Mex
sauce: combine 1/2 teaspoon each of garlic powder, onion powder, cumin, coriander, and
cayenne with 1 teaspoon mesquite liquid smoke and 1/4 cup each of ketchup, cider vinegar,
honey, and brown sugar.

teriyaki wings
Replace the paprika, chili powder, and celery seeds in the seasoning mix with 2 teaspoons
ground ginger and 2 teaspoons garlic powder. Replace barbecue sauce with teriyaki sauce.

spicy honey-garlic wings
Omit the chili powder, celery seeds, and barbecue sauce. Add 1 teaspoon each of ground
ginger and garlic powder. For the sauce, combine 1 cup clover honey, 1/2 cup corn syrup,
8 large pressed cloves of garlic, and 1 teaspoon crushed red pepper flakes. Heat the sauce
gently in a skillet and pour over the grilled wings.

variations

charcoal-grilled skewered shrimp

see base recipe page 19

margarita shrimp skewers
Replace marinade with a mixture of 1/2 cup tequila, 1/4 cup fresh orange juice,
2 tablespoons canola oil, and 1/2 cup fresh lime juice. Alternate with the shrimp on the
skewers 3 fresh jalapeños, cut into 1/2-inch slices, and 1 large red bell pepper, cut into
1/2-inch squares.

spicy grilled shrimp
Replace marinade with a mixture of 2 tablespoons each of olive oil, minced garlic,
Worcestershire sauce, and fresh lemon juice; 6 tablespoons melted unsalted butter;
2 teaspoons each of chili powder and freshly ground black pepper; and 1 teaspoon sea salt.

honey grilled shrimp
While grilling, baste unmarinated skewers with mixture of 1/2 cup each of clover honey and
fresh lime juice, grated zest of 1 lime, and 1 teaspoon each of sea salt and white pepper.

zesty grilled shrimp
Replace marinade with a mixture of 1 cup pineapple juice; 1/4 cup each of fresh lemon juice
and canola oil; 1 tablespoon soy sauce; and 1 teaspoon each of Louisiana hot sauce, celery
seeds, and sea salt.

grilled oysters san felipe

see base recipe page 20

grilled bay oysters

Omit crumb topping. Replace sauce with a mixture of 2 tablespoons unsalted butter; 1/2 small onion, minced; 1/2 cup chili sauce; 1 tablespoon each of clover honey and Worcestershire sauce; 6 dashes Tabasco sauce. Sauté till onion is soft, then cool before topping oysters.

hickory-smoked herb oysters

Replace sauce with a mixture of 4 tablespoons unsalted butter, 1/4 cup dry sherry, 2 large pressed cloves garlic, 2 teaspoons dried basil, and 1/4 cup finely chopped walnuts. Sauté till garlic is cooked, then cool before topping the oysters. Replace crumb topping with a squeeze of lemon juice over oysters and a sprinkle of freshly grated Parmesan cheese. Use 1 bag hickory chips for grill.

barbecued oysters with spicy garlic butter

Omit crumb topping. Replace sauce with a mixture of 12 tablespoons unsalted butter, 2 tablespoons chopped fresh parsley, 1 tablespoon each of fresh lemon juice and pressed garlic, 1 teaspoon each of grated lemon zest and Louisiana hot sauce. Sauté till garlic is cooked, then cool before topping oysters.

grilled oysters in the whole shell

Omit crumb topping and sauce. Do not open the oysters. Clean and grill until they open. Serve with Tabasco sauce or cocktail sauce.

variations

bacon wraps

see base recipe page 23

bacon-wrapped water chestnuts
Prepare the basic recipe, omitting the chicken livers, soy sauce, and sugar. Combine and simmer in a saucepan 2 cups ketchup and 2 tablespoons Worcestershire sauce. Pour this sauce over the grilled water chestnuts.

bacon-wrapped pineapple chunks
Prepare the basic recipe, omitting the chicken livers, soy sauce, and sugar, and replacing the water chestnuts with one 15-ounce can pineapple chunks.

bacon-wrapped dates
Prepare the basic recipe, omitting the chicken livers, soy sauce, and sugar, and replacing the water chestnuts with one container of seeded dates (approximately 60).

bacon-wrapped shrimp
Prepare the basic recipe, omitting the chicken livers, soy sauce, and sugar. Replace the water chestnuts with 1 pound medium shrimp, peeled and deveined (approximately 45), which have been seasoned with 2 teaspoons each of garlic powder and sea salt.

bbq sweet and spicy meatballs

see base recipe page 24

smoked Italian meatballs
Substitute mozzarella cheese for the Parmesan; replace raspberry jam with 1 cup Italian
tomato sauce.

barbecued teriyaki meatballs
Omit the cheese, oregano, and basil. Replace barbecue sauce and raspberry jam with teriyaki
sauce and ground ginger.

smoky cocktail meatballs
Omit the garlic, onion, oregano, and basil, and replace with three 1-ounce packs of dry onion
soup mix. Replace sauce with a combination of 2 cups ketchup, 1 cup packed light brown
sugar, and 1/4 cup Worcestershire sauce. Heat this sauce gently for 5 minutes and serve with
the grilled meatballs.

smoked grape jelly meatballs
Omit the garlic, onion, oregano, and basil. Replace the sauce with a combination of
1 1/2 cups chili sauce, 1 1/2 cups grape jelly, and 1 tablespoon Dijon mustard. Heat this
sauce gently for 5 minutes and serve with the grilled meatballs.

variations

grilled pizza

see base recipe page 26

italian pizza with goat cheese
Replace the mozzarella cheese and pepperoni with caramelized onions, goat cheese warmed to room temperature, and 1/2 cup chopped fresh basil.

halftime pizzas
Add to the toppings 1/2 cup cooked and crumbled Italian sausage and 4 slices Canadian bacon, chopped.

barbecued chicken pizza
Replace the Italian sauce with 1 cup barbecue sauce. Omit the pepperoni and replace with 1 1/2 cups barbecued chicken breast or cooked diced chicken, 1/4 cup chopped onion, and 1/2 cup canned mushroom stems and pieces.

"blt" pizza appetizer
Omit the Italian tomato sauce, pepperoni, peppers, and olives. Spread the pizza crust with 1/2 cup real mayonnaise and top with 8 to 10 slices cooked bacon, cut into quarters. After grilling, garnish with 1 cup torn romaine lettuce.

grilled quesadillas

see base recipe page 27

spicy gourmet grilled quesadillas
Add to the filling ingredients 1/2 cup sour cream; 4 scallions, white and green parts sliced thin; 1 ripe tomato, peeled, seeded, and finely diced; 1 to 2 jalapeño peppers, stemmed, seeded, and minced; and 1/4 cup chopped fresh cilantro.

grilled chicken quesadillas
Omit 4 ounces Monterey Jack cheese. Add 2 cups diced cooked or barbecued chicken, 1 medium sliced red onion, 4 ounces grated sharp cheddar cheese, 1/4 cup chopped fresh cilantro leaves, and 1 minced jalapeño.

grilled pulled pork quesadillas
Add 2 cups pulled or shredded pork, 1/4 cup finely sliced scallions, 1 cup barbecue sauce, 1 tablespoon cider vinegar, and 2 teaspoons basic barbecue rub (see page 12).

steak quesadillas
Add marinated grilled steak and your own fresh pico de gallo.

variations

tomato-basil bruschetta

see base recipe page 29

cheesy bruschetta

Omit tomato-basil mixture and Parmesan cheese. Spread grilled garlic slices with 4 ounces softened goat cheese or cream cheese. Garnish with 4 thinly sliced green onions and kosher salt to taste.

angel's bruschetta

Omit tomato-basil mixture and Parmesan cheese. Spread grilled garlic slices with a mixture of 1 minced medium onion, 1 pressed large clove garlic, 1/2 teaspoon each dried oregano and basil, salt to taste, and 8 ounces thinly sliced mozzarella cheese.

bruschetta with roasted peppers

Omit tomato-basil mixture and Parmesan cheese. Spread grilled garlic slices with a mixture of 2 medium roasted red peppers, diced; 2 cloves garlic, pressed; 2 anchovy fillets, diced; 1 tablespoon chopped Italian parsley; and salt and pepper to taste.

shrimp bruschetta

Omit tomato-basil mixture and Parmesan cheese. Spread grilled garlic slices with a mixture of 8 ounces cooked salad shrimp, 2 tablespoons olive oil, 1 tablespoon each of balsamic vinegar and lemon juice, 1/4 teaspoon garlic powder, and black pepper.

variations

thai chicken satay skewers

see base recipe page 30

s.k.'s malaysian satay
Replace chicken with 1 pound of pork tenderloin. For the marinade, replace soy sauce, lime juice, red pepper, and water with 1 cup finely minced shallots, 1 teaspoon each of ground coriander, salt, and cumin; and 1 tablespoon each of ground turmeric, sugar, and cooking oil.

rasa malaysian chicken satay
For the marinade, replace soy sauce, lime juice, ginger, and pepper flakes with 6 finely minced shallots, 4 tablespoons each of cooking oil and Kecap Manis (ABC brand from Indonesia recommended), 2 tablespoons each of minced lemongrass and oyster sauce, 2 teaspoons ground turmeric, and 1 teaspoon each of ground coriander and chili powder.

thai prawn satay
Replace chicken with 1 pound prawns. For the marinade, replace soy sauce, lime juice, ginger, pepper flakes, and water with 1 tablespoon each of palm sugar, soy sauce, white pepper, Golden Mountain sauce (or Maggi seasoning sauce), and oyster sauce, and 1 teaspoon Thai curry powder.

ratami's lamb satay
Replace chicken with 1 pound boneless leg of lamb. For the marinade, replace soy sauce, lime juice, ginger, pepper flakes, and water with 1 minced large shallot, 2 pressed cloves garlic, 2 tablespoons Kecap Manis, 2 tablespoons fresh lemon juice, 1 tablespoon palm sugar, 1 teaspoon tamarind paste dissolved in 1 tablespoon hot water, and salt and pepper to taste.

variations

marinated grilled artichokes

see base recipe page 32

grilled artichokes with lemon yogurt
Replace marinade with 3/4 cup olive oil, juice of 2 lemons, 1 tablespoon each of finely chopped garlic and chopped fresh parsley leaves, and salt and pepper to taste. Serve with lemon yogurt.

artichoke kebabs
Replace marinade with 2 tablespoons fresh lemon juice, 1/2 teaspoon dried thyme, and salt and pepper to taste. Thread artichoke leaves onto water-soaked bamboo skewers. Serve with mayonnaise or dipping sauce of your choice.

hitching post grilled artichokes
Replace marinade with grated zest of 2 lemons, 1/4 cup melted butter, 2 tablespoons each of dry white wine and fresh lemon juice, 2 teaspoons garlic salt, and freshly ground black pepper to taste. Serve with a spicy smoked-tomato mayonnaise.

citrus artichokes
Replace marinade with 1/2 cup chicken stock; 3 tablespoons melted unsalted butter; 2 tablespoons each of walnut oil and olive oil, and chopped flat-leaf parsley; 1 tablespoon each of lemon and orange juices, lemon and orange zest, and minced garlic; and salt and pepper to taste.

bacon-wrapped jalapeño poppers

see base recipe page 33

andouille-stuffed jalapeños
Omit the cheddar and brown sugar. Add 1/4 cup cooked and crumbled andouille; 4 green onions, sliced thin; 1 large clove garlic, pressed; and 1 tablespoon chopped fresh parsley.

pulled pork-stuffed jalapeños
Omit the cheeses and brown sugar. Add 1 cup minced pulled pork, 1 cup grated chipotle cheddar cheese, 1 tablespoon cider vinegar, and 2 teaspoons barbecue rub (see page 12).

armadillo eggs
Omit the cheeses and brown sugar. Add 1 pound mild pork sausage, cooked and crumbled; 1 tablespoon crushed red pepper flakes; and 1 tablespoon garlic salt.

crab-stuffed jalapeños
Omit the bacon, cheeses, and brown sugar. Add 1 pound lump crabmeat, 2 tablespoons minced sweet red pepper, 2 tablespoons grated onion, 1 minced large clove garlic, 1 tablespoon Dijon mustard, and salt and pepper to taste.

scallion-stuffed poppers
Omit the cheddar and bacon. Add 3/4 cup chopped scallions to make a cream cheese and scallion stuffing.

flaming fish
and shellfish

When it comes to barbecuing, there's little simpler

than a perfectly marinated piece of fish or shellfish,

popped on the grill until just cooked through.

brown sugar-cured salmon

see variations page 68

This quick-cure method enhances the natural sweetness of these succulent salmon fillets.

1 cup firmly packed light brown sugar
1 tbsp. Old Bay Seasoning
1 tbsp. curing salt
1 teaspoon freshly ground black pepper

Six 6- to 8-oz. salmon fillets, skin on
1/2 cup Dijon mustard
1/2 cup firmly packed light brown sugar

Combine the 1 cup brown sugar, Old Bay, curing salt, and pepper in a bowl and blend well.

Rinse the salmon under cold running water and pat dry with paper towels. Cover the fillets evenly on both sides with the sugar mixture. Wrap the fillets in plastic or put them in a nonreactive baking dish, cover, and let cure in the refrigerator for 2 hours.

Prepare an indirect fire at 230°F (110°C). Remove the fillets from the cure. Using a pastry brush paint the top of each fillet with mustard, place in the smoker (on some aluminum foil, for easy clean up), then top with the remaining 1/2 cup brown sugar. Cook until the white protein comes to the top of the fillets, which will take about 35 to 40 minutes. Serve hot.

Serves 6

grilled herby lemon salmon

see variations page 69

A gutsy Italian-style mixture of garlic and herbs is a perfect complement to rich salmon steaks.

1/4 cup balsamic vinegar
1/4 cup olive oil
1/4 cup fresh lemon juice
1 large clove garlic, pressed
1 tbsp. dried chives

1/2 tsp. ground thyme
1/8 tsp. ground rosemary
Sea salt and freshly ground black pepper to
    taste
Four 1-in.-thick salmon steaks

In a large bowl, combine all ingredients except the salmon; mix well. Add the salmon steaks to the bowl; spoon the marinade over them until they are well coated. Cover and refrigerate for at least 2 hours, turning the fish over after an hour.

Prepare a medium-hot grill. Remove the fish from the marinade and grill for 10 to 15 minutes, turning once halfway through cooking. Grill until the fish flakes easily with a fork.

Serves 6–8

"hot" grilled trout

see variations page 70

For this recipe you can use brook trout or any similar oily, freshwater fish.

1/4 cup fresh lemon juice
2 tbsp. unsalted butter, melted
2 tbsp. canola oil
2 tbsp. chopped fresh parsley
2 tbsp. sesame seeds

1 tbsp. Louisiana hot sauce
1 tsp. freshly grated gingerroot
1/2 tsp. sea salt
Four 1-lb. brook trout

In a shallow dish combine the lemon juice, butter, oil, parsley, sesame seeds, hot sauce, ginger, and salt; mix well.

Pierce the skin of the fish in several places with the tines of a fork. Roll the fish in the juice mixture to coat inside and out. Cover. Refrigerate for 30 minutes to 1 hour, turning occasionally. Remove the fish from the marinade; reserve the marinade. Place the fish in a wire grill basket sprayed with cooking spray; brush the fish with reserved marinade.

Prepare a medium-hot grill. Cook the fish for about 5 minutes. Turn; cook for 5 minutes longer. The fish is done when the flesh flakes easily.

Serves 4

grilled tilapia

see variations page 71

Tilapia, which originated in Africa, has recently begun to spread worldwide, winning many cooks over with its tender, creamy flesh.

3/4 cup mayonnaise
1 tsp. steak sauce
1 tsp. fresh lime juice
1 tsp. grated lime zest

2 tbsp. freshly grated Parmesan cheese
1/8 tsp. minced fresh dill
4 large tilapia fillets

Mix the mayonnaise, steak sauce, lime juice, lime zest, cheese, and dill. Spread generously on both sides of the tilapia fillets.

Place the coated fish on a preheated medium grill and cook for 3–5 minutes on each side or until the fish flakes easily with a fork.

Serves 4

grilled swordfish steaks with citrus salsa

see variations page 72

A vibrant Mexican-inspired salsa is a perfect accompaniment to meaty swordfish steaks.

1 cup picante sauce or chunky salsa
1 tsp. grated orange zest
2 tbsp. fresh orange juice
1 tbsp. chopped fresh cilantro

1 cup coarsely chopped orange
1 medium tomato, diced
2 green onions, sliced thin
4 swordfish steaks, 1 in. thick (about 1 1/2 lbs.)

Mix the picante sauce or salsa, orange zest, orange juice, and cilantro. Set aside 1/2 cup. Add orange, tomato, and onions to remaining picante sauce mixture to make the citrus salsa.

Grill the fish over medium heat for 10 minutes or until done, turning once, and brushing often with the reserved 1/2 cup picante sauce mixture. Serve the fish with the citrus salsa.

Serves 4

grilled halibut with pineapple

see variations page 73

Here is more proof that citrus and fish are the perfect marriage of flavors.

1 tbsp. grated lime zest
2 tbsp. fresh lime juice
2 tbsp. light brown sugar
2 tbsp. grated fresh gingerroot
1 tsp. sea salt

1/4 tsp. chipotle powder
Four 6-oz. halibut fillets cut 1/2-in. thick
1/2 medium pineapple, peeled and cut
   lengthwise into 1/2-in.-thick spears

Coat the grill with cooking spray and preheat. Place the zest, lime juice, 1 tablespoon brown sugar, 1 tablespoon ginger, salt, and chipotle powder in a resealable plastic bag; shake to combine. Add the fish to this bag. Reseal, shake again, place the bag on a plate, and marinate at room temperature for 20 minutes, turning once.

Meanwhile, in a second plastic bag, place the remaining brown sugar, ginger, and pineapple. Allow to marinate for 5 minutes; remove the pineapple and add any juices to the fish bag.

Grill the pineapple until heated through, turning once. Remove to a serving platter and cover with foil to keep warm. Remove the fish from its marinade. Cook the fish over direct heat until cooked through; allow 3 to 4 minutes per side. Place on a serving platter with the pineapple.

Serves 4

grilled shark to die for

see variations page 74

Shark steaks are delicious and widely available. The variety known as dogfish is particularly easy to find and would be suitable here.

1/2 cup soy sauce	2 tbsp. fresh lemon juice
1/2 cup fresh orange juice	1 tsp. freshly ground black pepper
1/4 cup ketchup	2 large cloves garlic, pressed
1/4 cup chopped fresh parsley	Six 6-oz. shark steaks

Combine soy sauce, orange juice, ketchup, chopped parsley, lemon juice, pepper, and garlic. Set aside 1/4 cup. Add the fish; cover and marinate in the refrigerator for 2 hours. Remove the fish from its marinade. Grill the fish over high heat on a preheated grill, basting frequently with the reserved 1/4 cup marinade, for 6 minutes on each side or until the fish flakes easily when tested with a fork

Serves 6

mexican grilled red snapper

see variations page 75

Achiote paste is a traditional Mexican ingredient with a salty, spicy flavor. You should be able to find it in any large supermarket.

1/2 cup achiote paste
1/2 cup orange juice
3 tbsp. fresh lemon juice
3 tbsp. fresh lime juice

Zest of 1 lemon and 1 lime
1 whole red snapper, split and butterflied
(about 2 lbs.)
Heated salsa

Mix the achiote paste with the citrus juices and zest. Cover all surfaces of the fish with the mixture. Place the fish in the refrigerator and leave to marinate for 30 minutes to 1 hour.

Place the fish on a grill preheated to medium, skin-side down. When the fish is about halfway done (after about 5 minutes), turn it and continue cooking for another 3 minutes. You should be able to lift the central bone out easily when the fish is cooked. Top with heated salsa.

The traditional Mexican way to cook fish is to place it on a banana leaf. If you can find it, wash the leaf and place it on the grill while it's still wet. Then add the fish. This is an old trick to keep the fish from sticking to the grill and falling apart when you try to turn it.

Serves 4–6

grilled citrus tuna

see variations page 76

Tuna steaks can become tough if not cooked carefully. Tenderize them in acidic fruit juices first, then cook them briefly to retain their melting texture.

1 cup orange juice
1 cup grapefruit juice
1/4 cup lime juice
1/2 cup dry sherry

1 tsp. dried thyme
1/4 tsp. cayenne pepper
1/4 tsp. sea salt
4 lbs. tuna steaks
1 tbsp. paprika

Mix the juices, sherry, thyme, cayenne, and salt in a shallow baking dish. Add the fish and allow to marinate for 30 minutes to 1 hour in the refrigerator. Remove the tuna from the marinade and discard the marinade. Place the fish on a grill preheated to high and sprinkle with paprika.

Turn after about 3 to 5 minutes and continue cooking for another 3 to 5 minutes. Allow more time if you like your fish well cooked.

Serves 4

beer and herb shrimp

see variations page 77

I like to serve these juicy shrimp with glasses of dark beer to complement the smoky flavors of the marinade.

2 lbs. peeled and deveined shrimp
1 1/2 cups dark beer
2 cloves garlic, pressed
2 tbsp. chopped fresh chives
2 tbsp. chopped fresh parsley

1 1/2 tsp. sea salt
1/2 tsp. freshly ground black pepper
Shredded lettuce
2 green onions, sliced thin

Combine all ingredients except the lettuce and green onions in a bowl. Cover and refrigerate for 3 to 4 hours, stirring occasionally. Drain.

Prepare a medium-hot grill. Place the shrimp in a heavy-bottomed skillet or wok and place over the grill. Cook the shrimp until pink and tender, about 2 minutes on each side, or less for small shrimp. Do not overcook or the shrimp will become tough. Serve the shrimp on shredded lettuce and sprinkle with sliced green onions.

Serves 8

citrus-grilled scallops

see variations page 78

You should remove the corals (roe) from your scallops before preparing this dish, but don't discard them: sautéed with butter and garlic they make a delicious snack.

1 cup water
1 cup chardonnay
1/4 cup fresh lemon juice
1 tbsp. unsalted butter
1 tbsp. clover honey
Pinch sea salt

1 clove garlic, pressed
2 tsp. cornstarch, dissolved in 2 tbsp. water
12 scallops, halved widthwise
Melted butter as needed
Chopped fresh parsley

In a small saucepan, combine the water, wine, lemon juice, butter, honey, salt, and garlic. Place over medium heat; reduce to almost half, stirring frequently. Add the cornstarch solution to thicken sauce to taste. Remove from heat; keep warm.

Grill the scallops over high heat for about 3 minutes a side, brushing frequently with melted butter. Cook to your desired doneness, but do not overcook. Remove the scallops from the grill. Place 6 scallop halves on each plate. Pour the citrus sauce over the scallops and garnish with parsley.

Serves 4

grilled catfish

see variations page 79

Catfish are named for their "whiskers." The flavor is far finer than this unappetizing name might suggest; catfish are valued by gourmets from the USA to Indonesia.

Six 6-oz. catfish fillets
1 tbsp. garlic salt

1 tsp. white pepper
2 to 3 tbsp. drawn butter or corn oil

Sprinkle the fish fillets with the garlic salt and pepper. Dip them in drawn butter and grill over hot coals until the fish flakes easily (about 4 to 6 minutes per side). Be very careful when turning as catfish is very delicate; you might consider using a wire grill basket. Serve with salsa, tartar sauce, or herbed mustard.

Serves 6

brown sugar-cured salmon

see base recipe page 47

lemon and basil salmon
Replace the brown sugar cure with 1 cup each of lemon yogurt and fresh basil leaves. Marinate for 2 hours and proceed to grill as in the base recipe.

mayonnaise and dill salmon
Replace the brown sugar cure with 1 cup real mayonnaise and 1 tablespoon dried dill. Marinate for 2 hours and proceed to grill as in the base recipe.

maple barbecued salmon
Omit the brown sugar cure. Grill the salmon as in the base recipe and serve with a sauce made by blending together 1/2 pound unsalted butter at room temperature and 1 cup maple syrup.

profanity salmon
Replace the brown sugar cure with 1/2 cup mayonnaise, 3 tablespoons teriyaki sauce, 1 teaspoon wasabi paste (you can substitute horseradish if desired), and salt and pepper to taste. Marinate for 2 hours and proceed to grill as in the base recipe.

juniper sugar-cured salmon
Prepare the base recipe, adding 2 teaspoons crushed juniper berries to the sugar cure.

variations

grilled herby lemon salmon

see base recipe page 48

tequila and lime grilled salmon steaks
Replace the marinade with a mixture of 1/2 cup tequila; 1/4 cup each of fresh lime juice, triple sec, extra-virgin olive oil, and freshly chopped cilantro; and 4 large cloves garlic, minced.

grilled teriyaki salmon steaks
Replace the marinade with a mixture of 1/2 cup each of soy sauce, sweet sherry or mirin, and sugar; and 1 teaspoon each ground ginger and dried garlic.

grilled salmon steaks with marmalade dijon marinade
Replace the marinade with a marmalade dijon marinade made by heating gently in a saucepan 1/2 cup orange marmalade, 1 tablespoon Dijon mustard, 1/2 teaspoon garlic powder, and 1/2 teaspoon ground ginger. Let cool, then marinade and grill salmon as in the base recipe.

salmon steaks with hoisin marinade
Replace the marinade with a hoisin marinade made by mixing 1/4 cup hoisin sauce, 2 tablespoons clover honey, 2 tablespoons fresh orange juice, and 1/4 teaspoon chipotle powder.

"hot" grilled trout

see base recipe page 51

cajun-grilled trout with apple salsa

Omit the marinade. Instead dust the trout with Cajun spice mix before grilling, and serve the cooked fish with apple salsa. Garnish with fresh herbs and lemon wedges.

sesame-grilled trout

Replace marinade with a mixture of 1/4 cup fresh lemon juice, 2 tablespoons unsalted butter, 3 tablespoons chopped fresh parsley, 2 tablespoons toasted sesame seeds, 1 tablespoon Tabasco sauce, and sea salt to taste.

grilled spicy trout

Replace the marinade with an Asian-flavored paste: mix 2 tablespoons fresh lemon juice; 1 tablespoon each of toasted ground cumin, chili powder, and canola oil; 1 teaspoon garam masala; and sea salt and freshly ground black pepper to taste. Pat this paste onto the fish before grilling.

grilled trout with thai sweet glaze

Replace the marinade with a Thai glaze; mix 6 tablespoons hoisin sauce, 3 tablespoons clover honey, 3 minced shallots, 2 tablespoons rice vinegar, 1 tablespoon Thai fish sauce, 1 tablespoon dark soy sauce, 1 tablespoon grated fresh gingerroot, 2 pressed large cloves garlic, and 1/4 teaspoon Chinese five-spice powder. Brush both sides of the fish with this glaze before cooking.

grilled tilapia

see base recipe page 52

grilled tilapia with spinach and cherry tomatoes
Prepare the base recipe. Make a vegetable garnish for the grilled tilapia. Sauté 1 thinly sliced scallion and 1 pound fresh spinach. Cook until wilted, then stir in 2 cups halved cherry tomatoes. Serve alongside the grilled fish.

african tilapia
Omit the lime and mayonnaise coating. Make an African-flavored marinade by combining 1 cup light olive oil; 1 small onion, chopped fine; 1 sweet red pepper, chopped; juice and zest of 1 lemon; 1 tablespoon vinegar; 2 teaspoons cayenne or crushed red pepper flakes; and 1 teaspoon sea salt. Marinate the tilapia for 2 hours, drain, and grill as in the base recipe .

spicy grilled tilapia with aïoli
Omit the lime and mayonnaise coating. Before grilling, rub the tilapia with 1 teaspoon each of garlic powder, onion powder, and toasted ground cumin, and 2 tablespoons chili powder. Make an aïoli by whisking together 1 1/2 cups mayonnaise, 6 pressed garlic cloves, 1/2 tablespoon lemon juice, 1 1/2 tablespoons Dijon mustard, and 3/4 teaspoon dried tarragon. Grill as in the base recipe.

lime and basil tilapia
Omit the lime and mayonnaise coating. Before grilling, marinate the tilapia for 2 hours in a mixture of 1/4 cup olive oil, the juice and zest of 2 limes, 1 tablespoon chopped fresh basil, 2 teaspoons bourbon, 1 teaspoon sea salt, and freshly ground black pepper to taste.

variations

grilled swordfish steaks with citrus salsa

see base recipe page 54

grilled swordfish with fresh tomato and herb salsa
Replace citrus salsa with a tomato salsa: mix 4 large plum tomatoes, peeled, seeded, and diced; 1/4 cup chopped fresh basil; 2 tablespoons chopped fresh marjoram; 1 minced shallot; 1 teaspoon cracked black pepper; and salt to taste.

grilled swordfish with roast red pepper
Omit the citrus baste and salsa. Instead, marinate swordfish for 2 hours in a mixture of 2 tablespoons fresh lemon juice and 1 cup olive oil. Grill as in the base recipe and, serve with 4 roasted red peppers, peeled, seeded, and cut into strips; 1 tablespoon chopped fresh parsley; and salt and pepper to taste.

grilled ginger swordfish
Omit the citrus baste and salsa. Instead, marinate swordfish for 2 hours in a mixture of 1/2 cup olive oil, 3 tablespoons soy sauce, 3 tablespoons dry sherry, and 1 tablespoon grated fresh gingerroot. Remove from marinade and grill as in the base recipe, brushing often with the marinade.

grilled dijon swordfish steaks
Omit the citrus baste and salsa. Marinate the swordfish for 2 hours in a mixture of 2 tablespoons Dijon mustard, 2 tablespoons olive oil, 1 tablespoon melted butter, and 1 tablespoon white wine vinegar. Remove from marinade and grill as in the base recipe, brushing often with the marinade. Serve with tartar sauce.

grilled halibut with pineapple

see base recipe page 55

grilled halibut with tomato, cucumber, and lemon sauce
Omit lime marinade and pineapple. Instead, whisk together 1 teaspoon grated lemon zest, 1 1/2 tablespoons fresh lemon juice, 1/2 teaspoon dried oregano, and 1/4 cup olive oil. Stir into this mixture 3/4 cup thinly sliced and seeded cherry tomatoes and 1/2 cup thinly sliced and seeded cucumber. Pour this sauce over the grilled halibut before serving.

grilled halibut with garlic butter
Omit lime marinade and pineapple. Instead, season the fish before cooking with a rub made from 1/2 teaspoon each of garlic powder, paprika, onion powder, lemon pepper, and salt. Mix together 3 tablespoons melted butter, 1 1/2 tablespoons olive oil, 1 tablespoon chopped fresh parsley, and 2 pressed cloves garlic. Brush this garlic butter over the fish before grilling.

grilled chinese halibut
Omit lime marinade and pineapple. Instead, combine 1 tablespoon grated fresh ginger, 3 chopped scallions, 2 tablespoons light soy sauce, 2 tablespoons Chinese rice wine or dry sherry, and 1 tablespoon each of dark soy sauce and Chinese sesame oil. Marinate halibut in this mixture for 2 hours before grilling. Garnish with 2 tablespoons chopped fresh cilantro.

grilled blue cheese halibut
Omit lime marinade and pineapple. Instead, combine 1/4 pound crumbled blue cheese, 2 cups buttermilk, 1 1/2 cups mayonnaise, and water to thin if needed. Reserve some of the marinade to use as a sauce. Garnish with 1 large red onion, sliced thin and grilled.

variations

grilled shark to die for

see base recipe page 57

anticucho-style grilled shark
Replace the marinade with a blend of 1/2 cup soy sauce; 2 pickled jalapeños; 2 tablespoons each of jalapeño juice, fresh cilantro, and parsley leaves; 1/4 cup fresh lime juice; 1/2 cup canola oil; and 1 teaspoon cracked black pepper. Proceed with the base recipe. Garnish the grilled steaks with lime wedges, avocado, and *pico de gallo*.

marinated grilled shark
Replace the marinade with a mix of 1/3 cup fresh lime juice, 1/4 cup teriyaki sauce, 2 tablespoons olive oil, 1 tablespoon light brown sugar, 1/2 teaspoon coarse ground black pepper, and 1/2 teaspoon paprika.

asian-grilled shark steak
Replace the marinade with a mix of 2 tablespoons soy sauce, 3 tablespoons fresh lemon juice, 2 tablespoons olive oil, 1 tablespoon sesame oil, 1 tablespoon yellow mustard, and 1 teaspoon sugar.

herbed shark steaks
Omit the marinade. Rub shark all over with 6 pressed garlic cloves. Combine 2 tablespoons lemon juice, 1 tablespoon fresh oregano leaves, 1 tablespoon chopped fresh parsley, 1 teaspoon fresh dill weed, and salt and pepper to taste. Marinate garlic-rubbed shark for 2 hours and drain. Grill as in the base recipe.

mexican grilled red snapper

see base recipe page 58

grilled red snapper
Replace the marinade with a mixture of 1/4 cup soy sauce, 2 teaspoons fresh lime juice,
1 tablespoon lemon pepper, 2 teaspoons garlic powder, and 1 teaspoon sea salt.

grilled snapper with shallot butter
Replace whole snapper with 2 pounds red snapper fillets, skin on. Replace marinade with a
mixture of 2 tablespoons olive oil, sea salt to taste, 1/2 teaspoon lemon zest, juice of 1/2 lemon,
2 tablespoons melted butter, 1 teaspoon dried tarragon, 1 tablespoon balsamic vinegar, 1 minced
large shallot, cracked black pepper to taste, and 1 pressed clove garlic. Grill as in the base recipe.

grilled red snapper with soy sauce and avocado
Replace fish with 2 pounds red snapper fillets. Marinate in a mixture of 1/4 cup fresh lemon
juice, 1 tablespoon grated fresh ginger, 5 pressed cloves garlic, and 1 minced large shallot. Grill
as in base recipe. Serve fish with a sauce made by blending together 1 tablespoon clover honey,
1 tablespoon soy sauce, 1/2 cup water, and 1 tablespoon tahini. Garnish with 1 diced avocado.

grilled red snapper with crunchy red relish
Prepare the base recipe. Serve the grilled fish with a relish: sauté 1 cup sweet diced red pepper,
1 cup diced white onion, and 2 cloves chopped garlic in 1/4 pound unsalted butter. Mix in
1/2 cup chopped toasted pecans; 1 cup plum tomatoes, peeled, seeded, and diced; 1 cup diced
pimiento, 1/4 cup picante sauce; 1/4 cup chopped fresh basil; 1 tablespoon red wine vinegar;
and kosher salt and black pepper to taste. Garnish with lemon wedges.

grilled citrus tuna

see base recipe page 61

seared tuna in wasabi sauce
Omit the citrus marinade. Grill the tuna as in the base recipe. Serve with a sauce made by sautéeing together 1 1/4 cups white wine, 2 tablespoons white wine vinegar, and 1/4 cup shallots, minced. Simmer until reduced to 1/4 cup. Strain out the shallots. Add 1 tablespoon each of wasabi paste and soy sauce. Stir in 1 cup butter, 1/2 cup chopped fresh cilantro, and 1/2 cup fresh minced parsley; serve with the grilled tuna.

grilled tuna in anchovy sauce
Omit the marinade. Grill the tuna as in the base recipe. Serve with an anchovy sauce made by heating gently together one 2-ounce can anchovies, drained; 10 black olives, pitted and chopped; 2 large cloves garlic, pressed; 1/4 cup white wine or chicken broth; 2 tablespoons chopped fresh parsley; 2 tablespoons fresh lemon juice; and 2 tablespoons capers, drained.

gourmet pepper-grilled tuna
Replace the citrus marinade with a pepper rub: brush the tuna with olive oil and then roll in a coating made from 1 tablespoon coarse ground tri-colored peppercorns, 1 tablespoon kosher salt, and 1 tablespoon grated lemon zest. Grill tuna as in the base recipe.

blackened tuna steaks
Replace the marinade with a mixture of 1/4 cup olive oil, 2 tablespoons fresh lime juice, and 1 tablespoon Dijon mustard. Replace paprika rub with 2 tablespoons dried cilantro, 1 tablespoon chili powder, and 1 teaspoon each of cracked black pepper and mustard seeds.

beer and herb shrimp

see base recipe page 62

herb-grilled shrimp
Replace marinade with a mixture of 1/4 cup Italian salad dressing, 1/4 cup olive oil, 4 pressed cloves garlic, 1 tablespoon each of chopped fresh basil and dried thyme, and chili sauce to taste.

grilled shrimp primavera
Cook the shrimp as directed, without marinating first. Serve with linguine, the sauce recipe below, and a mixture of grilled vegetables such as button mushrooms, bell peppers, and onions. For the pasta sauce, heat 3 cups canned tomatoes, 2 tablespoons unsalted butter, juice of 1/2 lemon, 1 tablespoon basil leaves, and 1/4 teaspoon each of black pepper, crushed red pepper flakes, and dried marjoram. Omit the lettuce and sliced onions.

simple grilled shrimp
Grill the shrimp as directed, without marinating first. Drizzle over the cooked shrimp a mixture of 1/2 cup melted butter, 3 tablespoons fresh lemon juice, 2 tablespoons Worcestershire sauce, 1 tablespoon Tabasco sauce or to taste, and 1/4 teaspoon cayenne pepper.

grilled acadian peppered shrimp
Replace marinade with a mixture of 1 cup melted butter; 1 clove garlic, pressed; 1/2 teaspoon each of ground bay leaf, ground rosemary, basil, oregano, salt, cayenne, nutmeg, and paprika; 1 tablespoon freshly ground black pepper; and 2 tablespoons fresh lemon juice.

variations

citrus-grilled scallops

see base recipe page 65

grilled scallop kabobs
Omit the citrus marinade. Thread the raw scallop halves onto water-soaked bamboo skewers, alternating them with pieces of red bell pepper, green bell pepper, and small whole onions. Before grilling, roll the kabobs in a mixture of 1 teaspoon *fines herbes* or Italian seasoning, 1 teaspoon lemon pepper, 1/2 teaspoon garlic powder, 1/4 teaspoon sea salt, and 2 tablespoons extra-virgin olive oil.

scallops grilled on rosemary
Replace citrus marinade with a rosemary marinade. Mix 2 tablespoons olive oil, 1 teaspoon chopped fresh rosemary, 2 pressed large cloves garlic, and sea salt and black pepper to taste. Grill marinated scallops on a bed of fresh rosemary sprigs. Garnish with lemon wedges.

grilled scallops with ham and basil
Omit the citrus marinade. Make a marinade by sautéing 1 roughly chopped chipotle pepper, 1 pressed large clove garlic, 2 tablespoons olive oil, and the juice of 3 limes. Thread the marinated scallops onto water-soaked skewers, alternating with basil leaves and strips of sliced ham.

caribbean scallops
Replace the citrus marinade with a rub made from 2 tablespoons onion powder; 1 teaspoon dry mustard; 1/2 teaspoon each of ground allspice, ground cinnamon, and crushed red pepper flakes; 1/4 teaspoon garlic powder; 1/4 cup olive oil; and salt to taste.

grilled catfish

see base recipe page 66

creole-grilled catfish
Omit everything except the catfish. Grill the fish as in the base recipe. Make a sauce for the
cooked fillets by blending together 8 tablespoons butter, melted; 1 large clove garlic, pressed;
1/4 cup olive oil; the juice of 1 lemon; 1 tablespoon Creole seasoning; and 1 teaspoon each
of white pepper and lemon pepper.

grilled smoky catfish
Omit everything except the catfish. Marinate the catfish for 2 hours in 1/3 cup soy sauce,
3 tablespoons canola oil, 1 clove garlic, pressed, and 1 teaspoon grated fresh gingerroot. Grill
the fish as in the base recipe.

grilled marinated catfish
Omit everything except the catfish. Marinate the catfish for 2 hours in 2 tablespoons
olive oil, 1 tablespoon red wine vinegar, 1 tablespoon grated onion, 1/2 teaspoon sea
salt, 1/4 teaspoon fine ground black pepper, and 1/4 cup canola oil. Grill the fish in the
base recipe.

barbecued catfish
Omit everything except the catfish. Marinate the fish in 1/3 cup bacon fat, 2 teaspoons
Worcestershire sauce, 1 teaspoon garlic powder, 1 teaspoon celery salt, and a dash of Tabasco
sauce. Grill the fish as in the base recipe and serve with 1 cup bottled barbecue sauce.

chargrilled chicken and poultry

Crisp-skinned and tender-fleshed poultry is one of

barbecue's greatest pleasures.

whole barbecued chicken

see variations page 102

A plump whole chicken (free-range if possible) cooks to tender perfection on the grill.

One 3 1/2- to 4 1/2-lb. whole chicken
for the marinade
1 cup Italian salad dressing
1/4 cup cider vinegar
1 tsp. garlic powder
1 tsp. sea salt
1/2 tsp. crushed red pepper flakes
for the rub
2 tbsp. sugar
2 tbsp. light brown sugar
2 tbsp. seasoned salt

1 tbsp. garlic salt
1 tbsp. celery salt
2 tbsp. paprika
2 tsp. chili powder
1 tbsp. fine grind black pepper
1 tsp. ground allspice
1/2 tsp. dried basil
1/4 tsp. dried tarragon
1/4 tsp. chipotle powder
for the glaze
2 cups barbecue sauce

Discard the neck and giblets from the chicken. Rinse the chicken inside and out, and pat dry with paper towels. Combine the marinade ingredients and blend well. Place the chicken in a plastic bag and pour the marinade over it. Marinate for 4 hours in the refrigerator. Meanwhile, combine the rub ingredients and blend well. Set aside.

Remove the chicken from the marinade. Blot the excess marinade with paper towels and season the chicken inside and out with the rub. Cook using the indirect method at 230°F to 250°F (110°C to 120°C), for 3 to 5 hours, depending on the size of the chicken. Glaze with barbecue sauce for the last 30 minutes of the cooking process.

Serves 6

herbed beer can chicken

see variations page 103

Steaming a chicken over a half-filled beer can infuse it with a delicious flavor.

for the rub
2 tbsp. sugar
2 tbsp. garlic salt
1 tbsp. paprika
1 tsp. dried thyme
1 tsp. ground black pepper
1 tsp. grated lemon zest

1/4 tsp. dried rosemary
1 whole chicken (4 to 5 lbs.)
One 12-oz. can beer (room temperature)
1 clove garlic, minced
1 sprig fresh rosemary, chopped
1 tsp. dried thyme

Combine all rub ingredients in a small mixing bowl and set aside. Remove the giblets and neck from the chicken. Sprinkle all over with rub, including inside the cavity. Open the can of beer and discard half of it. Place minced garlic, rosemary, and thyme in the can. Make sure to pierce two more holes into the top of beer can. Place chicken over the can.

Preheat the grill. Place the bird on the grill, balanced by the beer can. Grill over indirect medium heat for 2 1/2 to 3 1/2 hours or until the internal temperature of the thigh is 165°F to 180°F (75°C to 82°C).

Wearing barbecue mitts, carefully remove the chicken and the can from the grill, being careful not to spill the beer — it will be hot. Let the chicken rest for about 10 minutes before lifting it from the can. Discard the beer. Cut the chicken into serving pieces. Serve warm.

Serves 4

apple-raisin stuffed chicken thighs

see variations page 104

Stuffing chicken thighs is not difficult to do, and helps keep the meat tender and full of fruity flavor.

2 tbsp. raisins or prunes
1 tbsp. dark rum
1 firm cooking apple
1/2 cup diced onion
2 tsp. sugar
1/2 tsp. ground cinnamon
1/4 tsp. ground allspice
1 cup fresh whole wheat breadcrumbs
8 boneless chicken thighs (skin removed, if desired)
1/4 cup apple juice

Put the raisins or prunes in a small bowl and sprinkle with rum. Let the fruit stand for 20 minutes. Peel, core, and chop the apple. Heat a sprayed nonstick skillet. Sauté the onion and apple, covered, for about 5 minutes over medium heat, stirring frequently. Mix the sugar, cinnamon, and allspice together, and sprinkle over the apple mixture. Toss in the breadcrumbs and raisins or prunes. Divide the stuffing and fill pockets in chicken thighs, securing with toothpicks.

Prepare a medium-hot grill. Add some chunks of applewood if using a charcoal grill. Spray grill racks with nonstick spray. Brush the chicken with apple juice. Place chicken on the grill, skin-side down; cook until it browns, about 6 to 8 minutes. Turn over, brush on more apple juice, and cook for about 6 more minutes or until cooked through. The grilling time depends on the size and thickness of the thighs.

Serves 4

grilled cornish game hens

see variations page 105

Tender Cornish game hens are small enough that everyone can enjoy their own bird.

3 tbsp. olive oil
2 tsp. chili powder
2 tbsp. chopped fresh thyme
2 tbsp. onion powder
1 tsp. garlic powder

1 tbsp. kosher salt
1/2 tsp. ground black pepper
Four 1 1/2- to 2-lb. Cornish game hens, each
    cut in half lengthwise

Mix the oil and seasonings in a small bowl to form a paste. Brush the paste over the hens. Marinate for 30 minutes at room temperature.

Grill the hens on a barbecue preheated to medium until cooked through and the juices run clear when a fork is stuck into the meat. Transfer to a platter and serve.

Serves 4

grilled herbed duck breasts

see variations page 106

The natural oil in duck breasts means they withstand perfectly the searing heat of a grill.

1/2 cup olive oil
Juice of 1 lemon
4 juniper berries, crushed
1 tbsp. Worcestershire sauce
2 cloves garlic, pressed
1 tsp. dried thyme

1 tsp. ground bay leaves
1/2 tsp. onion powder
1/2 tsp. black pepper
1/4 tsp. paprika
4 duck breasts

Put all ingredients except the duck breasts in a small saucepan. Simmer for about 5 to 7 minutes. Remove the mixture from the heat and allow to cool. Place the duck breasts in a resealable plastic bag. Pour 1/2 the cooled herb mixture over the duck, seal the bag, and allow to marinate in refrigerator for 6 to 8 hours. Reserve the remaining marinade.

Preheat the grill to medium-high. Remove duck breasts from their plastic bag, discarding the marinade. Place the duck on a lightly oiled grill grate. Allow to grill for 3 minutes, baste with the reserved quarter of the marinade mixture, and turn. Continue to cook, basting every 3 minutes, until the internal temperature of the breasts reaches 145°F (63°C). Remove from the heat, slice, and serve.

Serves 6

hot and sticky summertime chicken

see variations page 107

Here's an easy recipe for spatchcocked — split and grilled — chicken.

One 3 1/2- to 4 1/2-lb. whole chicken
for the marinade
One 12-oz. can Dr. Pepper
10 cloves garlic, pressed
3 whole chilies
2 tbsp. Louisiana hot sauce
1/2 cup grated onion
2 tbsp. chopped fresh cilantro

2 tbsp. chopped fresh parsley
2 tsp. sea salt
for the glaze
1/2 cup clover honey
2 tbsp. Dijon mustard
2 tbsp. grated fresh gingerroot
1 tbsp. grated orange zest
1 tbsp. grated lime zest

Remove the neck and giblets from inside the chicken. Rinse and dry the chicken. Spatchcock it by cutting down the length of the spine with a sharp knife and removing the backbone. In the center of the breast on the inside is a white piece of gristle, on the keel bone. Cut into the center of it, place your thumbs on either side of the breast, and pop out the keel bone. Flatten the bird. Place in a 1-gallon resealable plastic bag. Combine the marinade ingredients in a bowl. Pour over the chicken and seal the bag. Refrigerate for a minimum of 3 hours, though overnight is better.

In a small bowl, combine the glaze ingredients. Preheat the barbecue to medium heat. Place the bird on the grill, bone-side down. Discard the bag and the marinade. Cook the chicken for approximately 15 to 20 minutes on each side. When its internal temperature reaches 165°F (75°C), start to brush on the glaze. Continue brushing on the glaze until it is used up and the meat reaches 170°F (77°C). Remove the chicken from the grill and let sit for 10 minutes before cutting.

Serves 4

grilled turkey tenderloins with rosemary marinade

see variations page 108

Turkey brushed with a mellow herbed marinade is a perfect barbecue dish for fall.

2 green onions, sliced thin
1/2 cup fresh orange juice
3 tbsp. olive oil
2 tbsp. minced fresh rosemary leaves
2 tbsp. balsamic vinegar

1 tsp. grated lemon zest
2 tsp. lemon juice
1 tbsp. clover honey
1/2 tsp. sea salt
4 turkey tenderloins

Mix all ingredients except the turkey in a resealable plastic bag. Remove 1/4 cup and set aside. Add the turkey tenderloins to the marinade in the bag, seal, and shake to mix.

Marinate the turkey for at least one hour. Remove the turkey from the marinade and place on a grill rack over medium heat. Grill for 5 minutes and turn to grill the other side for an additional 3 to 5 minutes. Brush the turkey with the reserved 1/4 cup marinade during grilling. Remove from the grill and serve.

Serves 4

honey-citrus chicken

see variations page 109

Avoid the potential blandness of chicken breasts by marinating them in this simple sweet and sour mixture for an hour or so before cooking.

4 chicken breast halves
Juice of 1 orange
Juice of 1 lime
Juice of 1 lemon

3 tbsp. honey
2 tbsp. olive oil
1/2 tsp. Tabasco Chipotle Sauce

Gently pound the chicken breasts between sheets of plastic wrap with your hand or a meat mallet, just enough to make the breasts even in thickness. Marinate the meat in the citrus juices, honey, oil, and Tabasco for about an hour at room temperature.

Grill the chicken on a grill preheated to medium for about 5 to 7 minutes per side, turning once, or until cooked through. When pierced with a fork, the juices will run clear.

Serves 4

barbecued quail

see variations page 110

Plump little quails are always succulent. Serve them with wedges of lemon to add a sharp note to the predominantly sweet marinade.

1 cup finely sliced scallions
1/4 cup clover honey
2 tbsp. Worcestershire sauce
4 large cloves garlic, pressed
1 tbsp. dry mustard

2 tsp. chili powder
1 cup Chablis
Sea salt and freshly ground black pepper to taste
Four 4- to 5-oz. semiboneless quail

Combine all ingredients except the quail in a saucepan. Heat for about 15 minutes over medium heat. Remove from the heat and cool to room temperature.

Place the quail in a nonreactive baking dish and pour about two-thirds of the sauce over them. Reserve the rest of the sauce for basting while grilling. Preheat a grill to medium.

Marinate quail for about 30 minutes at room temperature and then grill for about 3 to 4 minutes on each side, basting regularly with the reserved third of the sauce. Remove when the flesh is firm and the juices run clear from the leg when pierced. Serve at once.

Serves 2

peach-ginger turkey cutlets

see variations page 111

Turkey cutlets are low in fat, so they are an excellent choice for those who want to eat healthily.

1 tbsp. finely grated gingerroot
3 tbsp. soy sauce
1/3 cup rice vinegar

1/3 cup olive oil
1/4 cup peach jam
Four 6-oz. turkey cutlets

Mix all ingredients except the turkey together for a marinade. Reserve 1/4 cup for basting. Place the cutlets and the rest of the marinade in a large resealable bag or baking dish. Refrigerate for 30 minutes, turning occasionally.

Heat and lightly oil the grill. Drain the cutlets. Grill for 5 minutes on each side, basting occasionally with the reserved marinade, until cooked thoroughly and the cutlets have reached an internal temperature of 170°F (77°C).

Serves 4

hot jamaican jerk chicken

see variations page 112

The jerk spice paste here is exceptionally fiery; you might want to use fewer chilies.

10 large Scotch bonnet chilies
3 scallions, chopped
2 tbsp. white wine vinegar
2 tbsp. dried rosemary
2 tbsp. dried basil
2 tbsp. dried thyme

2 tbsp. mustard seeds
2 tbsp. dried parsley
1 tsp. fresh lime juice
1 tsp. yellow mustard
Sea salt and black pepper to taste
12 chicken drumsticks

Purée the chilies, scallions, and all the other ingredients, except chicken, into a paste. Refrigerate for 2 hours. Submerge the chicken legs in the mixture and be sure they are well coated. Then grill the chicken legs over a very low heat for 40 to 50 minutes.

Or, to cook direct, cook on a grill preheated to medium, for 10 minutes per side or until the skin is crispy and golden brown. The legs are done when the juices run clear when pierced in the thickest part. Remove from the grill and tent with foil. Let rest for 5 minutes before serving.

Serves 4

turkey drumsticks with fruity salsa

see base recipe page 113

This Mexican-style salsa adds a zesty and intriguing note to the simply grilled turkey.

for the marinade
1/2 cup fresh lime juice
1/4 cup fresh chopped sage
3 tbsp. champagne wine vinegar
2 tbsp. sugar
1/2 cup olive oil
6 small turkey drumsticks
for the salsa
1 small pineapple, peeled and diced

1/4 cup jicama, peeled and diced
1 small papaya, peeled and diced
1 medium lime, peeled and diced
1 small red bell pepper, seeded and diced
1/2 cup diced red onion
1/4 cup finely chopped serrano chilies
1/4 cup chopped fresh cilantro
3 tbsp. fresh lime juice
Sea salt to taste

Combine lime juice, sage, vinegar, sugar, and oil in a small mixing bowl. Place the turkey in a large resealable plastic bag, pour the marinade over the turkey, and marinate overnight in the refrigerator. Remove the turkey from the marinade. Cook the turkey pieces on a preheated and lightly oiled grill, turning every 10 to 15 minutes. The turkey is cooked when the juices run clear or when the internal temperature reaches 170°F (77°C).

Meanwhile, combine pineapple, jicama, papaya, lime, pepper, and onion in a bowl. Stir in chilies, cilantro, lime juice, and salt. Serve as an accompaniment to the turkey.

Serves 6

variations

whole barbecued chicken

see base recipe page 81

moroccan-style smoked chicken
Replace the rub with a glaze made from 4 tablespoons melted unsalted butter, 1/4 cup
clover honey, 2 teaspoons ground ginger, 1 teaspoon ground cinnamon, 1 teaspoon ground
coriander, 1/4 teaspoon ground turmeric, 1/8 teaspoon ground mace, and sea salt and freshly
ground black pepper to taste.

marinated barbecued chicken
Replace the rub with a marinade made by mixing 1 cup soy sauce, 1/2 cup cider vinegar,
2 pressed cloves garlic, and 1 teaspoon each dried oregano leaves and tarragon leaves.

billy's barbecued chicken
Replace the rub with the following rub mixture: 1 tablespoon brown sugar; 1 tablespoon
paprika; 1 teaspoon each of onion salt, garlic salt, celery salt, and dry mustard; and
1/4 teaspoon cayenne pepper.

spicy barbecued chicken
Replace the rub with the following rub mixture: 1 cup light brown sugar; 1 tablespoon
ground allspice; and 1 teaspoon each of ground thyme, dry mustard, garlic powder, ground
ginger, and cayenne pepper.

herbed beer can chicken

see base recipe page 82

root beer can chicken barbecue
Substitute the following rub mixture: 1 tablespoon paprika, 1 teaspoon dry mustard,
1 teaspoon each of onion powder and sea salt, and 1/2 teaspoon each of garlic powder,
ground coriander, ground cumin, and freshly ground black pepper. Replace the beer can with
a 12-ounce can of root beer or Dr. Pepper.

stout beer can chicken barbecue
Substitute the following rub mixture: 1/4 cup firmly packed dark brown sugar; 1/4 cup sweet
paprika; 2 tablespoons ground black pepper; sea salt to taste; 1 tablespoon hickory salt;
2 teaspoons each of garlic powder, onion powder, and celery seeds; and 1 teaspoon chipotle
powder. Replace the beer can with a 12-ounce can of stout.

sweet california beer can chicken barbecue
Substitute the following rub mixture: 2 tablespoons light brown sugar, 1 tablespoon each
of sugar and smoked paprika, 1 1/2 teaspoons garlic powder, sea salt to taste, 1 teaspoon
pepper, 1/2 teaspoon dry mustard, and 1/4 teaspoon each of cayenne pepper, dried ground
sage, and poultry seasoning. Replace the beer with a beer can half-filled with white wine.

cola can chicken barbecue
Substitute the following rub mixture: 1 teaspoon each of dry mustard, sea salt, garlic
powder, pepper, and onion powder, and 1 tablespoon paprika. Replace the beer can with a
12-ounce can cola.

variations

apple-raisin stuffed chicken thighs

see base recipe page 85

grilled cajun chicken

Omit the apple-raisin stuffing. Instead, marinate the chicken thighs in 1/4 cup canola oil, 2 tablespoons Cajun spice mix, and sea salt and freshly ground black pepper to taste. Omit the apple juice, and glaze with 2 cups barbecue sauce.

oriental grilled chicken thighs

Omit the apple-raisin stuffing. Instead, marinate the thighs in 1 cup soy sauce, 1/2 cup dark brown sugar, 2 tablespoons peeled and chopped fresh ginger, 4 pressed large garlic cloves, and 1 teaspoon Chinese five-spice powder.

chipotle-lime grilled chicken thighs

Omit the apple-raisin stuffing. Instead, marinate the thighs in 1/2 cup fresh lime juice; 1/2 cup olive oil; 2 tablespoons canned chipotle peppers in adobo sauce, seeded and minced; 1 tablespoon clover honey; and salt and freshly ground black pepper to taste.

hot and sticky grilled thighs with apricot glaze

Omit the apple-raisin stuffing and the apple juice. Instead, glaze the thighs as they cook with an apricot glaze. Warm gently together 1 cup pureed apricot preserves, 1/2 cup champagne vinegar, 2 tablespoons light rum, 2 tablespoons hot mustard, and 2 pressed large garlic cloves.

variations

grilled cornish game hens

see base recipe page 86

citrus marinated cornish hens
Replace the spice paste with a marinade made by mixing 2 tablespoons olive oil, 1/2 cup fresh orange juice, 1/4 cup fresh lemon juice, 1/4 cup water, 1/3 cup minced onions, 1 teaspoon crumbled dried rosemary, 1/2 teaspoon dried thyme, and 1 pressed clove garlic. Let hens marinate for 2 hours.

john's grilled cornish game hens
Replace the spice paste with a rub made from 1 tablespoon garlic salt, 1 tablespoon lemon pepper, and 1 teaspoon poultry seasoning.

grilled cornish hens with tarragon and dijon mustard
Replace the spice paste with a marinade made from 1/2 cup buttermilk, 3 tablespoons Dijon mustard, 2 tablespoons white wine vinegar, 2 chopped shallots, 1 tablespoon gin, and 2 teaspoons dried tarragon. Let hens marinate for 2 hours. Remove from marinade and grill. Sprinkle the grilled hens with salt and pepper to taste.

mexican grilled cornish hens
Replace the spice paste with a rub made from 1/4 cup brown sugar; 1 tablespoon smoked paprika; 2 teaspoons chili powder; 2 teaspoons ground cumin; 1 teaspoon each of ground Mexican oregano, sea salt, onion powder, and cayenne pepper; 1/2 teaspoon garlic powder; and 1/2 teaspoon lemon pepper.

variations

grilled herbed duck breasts

see base recipe page 89

asian grilled duck breasts
Replace the marinade with an Asian-flavored one made by mixing 1/2 cup soy sauce, 1/4 cup red wine or cider, 2 tablespoons olive oil, 2 tablespoons light brown sugar, 1 tablespoon each of lemon juice and lime juice, 1/4 teaspoon garlic powder, 1/8 teaspoon ground black pepper, and sea salt.

grilled duck breast with ginger, balsamic vinegar, and orange sauce
Omit the marinade. Grill unmarinated duck breasts, then serve with a sauce made by mixing 1/2 cup fresh orange juice, 1 1/2 cups chicken stock, 1/4 cup balsamic vinegar, 2 teaspoons grated fresh gingerroot, 4 tablespoons melted butter, 1/2 teaspoon sea salt, 1 teaspoon cracked black pepper, and 1 teaspoon grated orange zest.

grilled duck breasts with plum glaze
Omit the herb marinade. Make a glaze by heating gently in a saucepan 1/4 cup unsalted butter, 1 tablespoon garlic salt, 2 teaspoons coarse ground black pepper, 1 cup red plum jelly, 1 cup hoisin sauce, 1 tablespoon grated fresh gingerroot, 1 teaspoon sea salt, and 1/2 teaspoon fine grind black pepper. Brush glaze onto breasts as they cook.

chargrilled duck breasts with redcurrant glaze
Omit the herb marinade. Before grilling, top each duck breast with 1 slice apple-smoked bacon. Make a glaze by heating gently in a saucepan 2 beef bouillon cubes, 1 cup water, 2 tablespoons redcurrant jelly, 1/2 teaspoon dry mustard, 1 tablespoon sherry or brandy, 1/8 teaspoon dried marjoram, 1/4 teaspoon dried oregano, and the grated zest of an orange.

hot and sticky summertime chicken

see base recipe page 90

oriental marinated smoked chicken
Replace the marinade with one made by combining 1/2 cup rice wine, 1/4 cup sesame oil, 1/4 cup soy sauce, 2 tablespoons honey mustard, 1/3 cup brown sugar, 2 dashes liquid smoke flavoring, 1 tablespoon grated orange zest, 2 teaspoons ground ginger, 2 teaspoons paprika, 1 teaspoon *fines herbes*, and 1/4 teaspoon ground rosemary.

mary's barbecued chicken
Replace the marinade with a rub made by mixing together 1 tablespoon sugar, 1 tablespoon fine-grain natural sugar, 2 tablespoons sea salt, 1 teaspoon each of dry mustard and onion powder, and 1/2 teaspoon each of paprika, dried cilantro, dried basil, garlic powder, ground coriander, ground cumin, and freshly ground black pepper.

peruvian grilled chicken
Replace the summertime marinade with one made by combining 1/3 cup soy sauce, 2 tablespoons canola oil, 2 tablespoons fresh lime juice, 5 large pressed cloves garlic, 2 teaspoons toasted ground cumin, 1 tablespoon paprika, and 1 teaspoon dried Mexican oregano.

easy grilled cajun chicken
Replace the summertime marinade with a rub made by mixing together 2 tablespoons smoked paprika, 1 tablespoon garlic powder, 2 teaspoons sea salt, and 1 teaspoon each of cayenne pepper, white pepper, black pepper, oregano, thyme, and onion powder.

variations

grilled turkey tenderloins with rosemary marinade

see base recipe page 91

turkey tenderloins with sherry and lemon marinade
Substitute for the rosemary marinade a blend of 1/4 cup each of soy sauce, olive oil, and sherry; 2 tablespoons each of fresh lemon juice and grated onion; 1/2 teaspoon ground ginger; pepper to taste; and a dash of seasoned salt.

tarragon turkey tenderloins
Substitute for the rosemary marinade a blend of 1/3 cup olive oil, 2 tablespoons red wine vinegar, 1 tablespoon Dijon mustard, 1 large pressed clove garlic, 2 teaspoons crushed dried tarragon, 1/2 teaspoon salt, and 1/4 teaspoon ground pepper.

plum-glazed szechwan turkey tenderloins
Substitute for the rosemary marinade a glaze made by heating gently together 1 cup plum jelly, 1/4 cup hoisin sauce, 2 tablespoons light brown sugar, 2 tablespoons triple sec, 1 tablespoon grated fresh ginger, 1/2 teaspoon habañero powder, 1 teaspoon kosher salt, 1 teaspoon ground Szechwan peppercorns, 1/2 teaspoon garlic powder, and 2 tablespoons canola oil.

hoisin-glazed turkey tenderloins
Substitute for the rosemary marinade a glaze made by heating gently together 1/4 cup hoisin sauce, 1/4 cup fresh orange juice, 1 teaspoon garlic powder, 1 teaspoon onion powder, and 1/2 teaspoon each of sea salt, freshly ground black pepper, and cayenne pepper.

variations

honey-citrus chicken

see base recipe page 92

afghan chicken
Replace the marinade with an Afghan version, made by mixing 2 large pressed cloves garlic, 1/2 teaspoon sea salt, 2 cups plain whole-milk yogurt, 4 tablespoons lemon juice, pulp of 1 large lemon, and 1/2 teaspoon cracked black pepper. Serve chicken with pita bread.

apple-honey glazed chicken
Replace the marinade with a glaze made by mixing 1/3 cup apple jelly, 1 tablespoon clover honey, 1 tablespoon Dijon mustard, 1/2 teaspoon ground cinnamon, and sea salt to taste.

athenian chicken on the grill
Replace the marinade with a Greek version, made by mixing 1/2 cup dry red wine; 1/2 cup olive oil; 1/4 cup fresh lemon juice; 2 tablespoons dried oregano; 1 teaspoon each of dried thyme, dried basil leaves; grated lemon zest; sea salt; and 1/2 teaspoon ground black pepper.

grilled italian chicken breasts
Replace the marinade with an Italian version, made by mixing 2 pressed cloves garlic, 1 teaspoon toasted and crushed fennel seeds, 2 tablespoons fresh lemon juice, 2 tablespoons olive oil, and sea salt and freshly ground black pepper to taste.

variations

barbecued quail

see base recipe page 95

grilled quail with jalapeño plum sauce

Replace the sauce with glaze: 2 1/2 tablespoons canola oil; 1/3 cup minced red onions, 1 1/2 tablespoons pressed garlic; 1/2 jalapeño pepper, chopped finely, 1 1/2 pounds purple plums, pitted and diced; 2 teaspoons mild curry powder; 1/2 teaspoon ground allspice; 1/2 cup clover honey; 1/4 cup soy sauce; and the juice of 1 orange and 2 lemons. Heat all glaze ingredients gently in pan.

grilled quail

Replace the sauce with marinade. Mix 1 tablespoon each chopped garlic and crushed juniper berries; juice of 1 lemon, 1/4 cup dry vermouth, 1/2 teaspoon dried thyme, 2 teaspoons rubbed sage, and sea salt and black pepper to taste. Marinate for 30 minutes. Glaze grilled quail with 4 tablespoons melted unsalted butter and 1 cup barbecue sauce, stirred together.

zesty garlic-lime quail

Replace the sauce with a spice paste made by combining 4 large pressed cloves garlic, 2 tablespoons light olive oil, 1 tablespoon grated lime zest, 2 teaspoons chopped fresh thyme leaves, and salt and pepper to taste. Rub into the quail and marinate for 30 minutes.

asian grilled quail

Replace the sauce with a marinade made by combining 1/4 cup hoisin sauce; 3 tablespoons each of chili-garlic sauce, dark sesame oil, and clover honey; 2 tablespoons sesame seeds; 1 teaspoon ground ginger; and 1/2 teaspoon Chinese five-spice powder. Marinate for 30 minutes.

peach-ginger turkey cutlets

see base recipe page 96

grilled mustard turkey cutlets
Replace the marinade with a sauce made by combining in a small bowl 2 tablespoons Dijon mustard, 2 teaspoons mayonnaise, 1 teaspoon fresh lemon juice, and pepper to taste. Garnish with a sprinkling of paprika and 2 tablespoons chopped fresh parsley.

grilled turkey scallopini with dijon sauce
Replace the marinade with a mustard version made by combining 1/4 cup canola oil, 1/4 cup clover honey, 2 tablespoons Dijon mustard, 1 teaspoon lemon zest, 2 tablespoons lemon juice, 1 pressed clove garlic, 1/4 teaspoon dried thyme, and sea salt and freshly ground black pepper to taste. Reserve 1/4 cup marinade to use as a sauce.

teriyaki turkey cutlets
Replace the marinade with an Asian version made by combining 1/2 cup soy sauce, 1/4 cup sweet rice wine, 2 tablespoons clover honey, 2 teaspoons grated fresh gingerroot, 1 teaspoon grated orange zest, 1 teaspoon sesame oil, and 2 cloves pressed garlic. Garnish with toasted sesame seeds.

spicy grilled turkey cutlets with grilled pineapple rings
Replace the marinade with a Caribbean version made by combining a 20-ounce can pineapple rings in juice, 3 tablespoons honey, 1 tablespoon vegetable oil, 1/4 teaspoon ground cinnamon, 2 tablespoons each of Jamaican jerk seasoning and soy sauce, 1 tablespoon each of lemon juice and dried onion, and 1/4 teaspoon salt. Use to baste turkey.

variations

hot jamaican jerk chicken

see base recipe page 99

maple-barbecued chicken drumsticks
Instead of making the spice paste, glaze the chicken with the following mixture, which you have warmed gently in a saucepan: 1/2 cup chili sauce, 1/2 cup maple syrup, 3 tablespoons cider vinegar, 3 tablespoons canola oil, 1 tablespoon prepared mustard, 1/2 teaspoon sea salt, and 1/4 teaspoon Louisiana hot sauce.

grilled chicken drumsticks
Instead of making the spice paste, marinate the chicken for 2 hours in the following mixture: 1/4 cup soy sauce, 1/4 cup fresh lemon juice, 1/4 cup sesame oil, 1/2 cup clover honey, 4 pressed cloves garlic, 2 tablespoons grated fresh gingerroot, 3 tablespoons canola oil, 1 teaspoon dried chili flakes, and pepper to taste.

simple grilled drumsticks
Instead of making the spice paste, rub the chicken with the following mixture before grilling: 4 teaspoons sea salt, 2 teaspoons smoked paprika, 1 teaspoon onion powder, and 1/2 teaspoon each of ground thyme, garlic powder, dried basil, and freshly ground pepper.

butch's lip-smacking chicken drumsticks
Instead of making the spice paste, marinate the chicken for 1 hour in the following mixture: 2 tablespoons ketchup; 2 tablespoons soy sauce; 1 tablespoon each of balsamic vinegar, clover honey, light brown sugar, and Dijon mustard; the juice and zest of 1 orange; and sea salt and freshly ground black pepper to taste.

variations

turkey drumsticks with fruity salsa

see base recipe page 100

mexican turkey drumsticks
Replace the salsa with a rub made from 2 teaspoons each of sea salt, fine grind black pepper, and chili powder, and 1/2 teaspoon each of ground cumin and garlic powder.

drumsticks in sweet and spicy barbecue sauce
Omit the salsa. Gently heat together 2 tablespoons light brown sugar, 1 cup ketchup, 1/4 cup fresh lemon juice, 1 tablespoon each of onion powder and Worcestershire sauce, 1 tablespoon Dijon mustard, and 1 teaspoon each of chili powder and cayenne pepper.

ginger-garlic barbecued turkey drumsticks
Omit the salsa. Gently heat together 1/2 cup light soy sauce, 2 tablespoons each of sherry and light brown sugar, 1 tablespoon grated gingerroot, 2 teaspoons oil, and 1 clove pressed garlic.

grilled turkey drumsticks
Omit the salsa. Gently heat together 1/4 cup fresh lemon juice; 2 tablespoons dark brown sugar; 1 tablespoon each of Worcestershire sauce, soy sauce, and Dijon mustard; 1 teaspoon each of chili powder and onion powder, 1/2 teaspoon chipotle powder; and 1 cup ketchup.

grilled buttermilk turkey drumsticks
Omit marinade and salsa. Instead, marinate drumsticks for at least 2 hours in mix of 2 cups buttermilk; 3 tablespoons each of Dijon mustard and clover honey; 2 teaspoons each of dried basil and sea salt; and 1/2 teaspoon each of dried thyme, dried oregano, dried dill, and black pepper.

perfect pork and lamb

Succulent meaty grills are often regarded as the centerpiece of a good barbecue — and here are dozens of superb choices. The recipes in this chapter will help you make the most of the sweet taste of pork and the smoky flavor of lamb.

teriyaki pork burgers

see variations page 139

In Japanese, *teri* means "sunshine" and *yaki* means "roast" or "grilled," so what could be more suitable for barbecuing?

1 1/2 lbs. ground pork
1/4 cup fine dry breadcrumbs
1/4 tsp. freshly ground black pepper
2 tbsp. finely chopped onion
2 green onions, sliced thin

1 large clove garlic, pressed
2 tbsp. soy sauce
2 tbsp. orange juice concentrate
2 tsp. ground ginger
1 tbsp. light brown sugar

Combine all the ingredients. Form into 4 to 6 patties. Grill over medium heat for 5 to 10 minutes per side or until no pink remains. Always cook ground pork to well done or 165°F (75°C). Serve on hamburger buns with your favorite condiments and garnish.

For a new taste sensation, serve on a hamburger or kaiser bun with a layer of oranges, sliced kiwifruit, and sliced strawberries on top.

Makes 4–6 burgers

jerk barbecued ribs

see variations page 140

Caribbean jerk seasoning adds a zesty kick to pork ribs.

1/2 cup Jamaican jerk seasoning
1 tbsp. light brown sugar
2 tbsp. red wine vinegar
4 lbs. pork spareribs
2 cups barbecue sauce

Combine the jerk seasoning, sugar, and vinegar in a bowl. Remove 1/4 of the mixture and reserve. Add the ribs to the remaining marinade in the bowl and turn to coat thoroughly. Marinate for 3 to 4 hours or overnight in the refrigerator. Remove ribs from marinade.

Heat a grill to medium. Cook ribs for 2 to 2 1/2 hours, turning and brushing frequently with the reserved 1/4 of the marinade. Brush and glaze the ribs with the barbecue sauce during the last 15 minutes of cooking.

Serves 6

german-style barbecued pork sandwich

see variations page 141

Slathered with mustard and served with crunchy pickles, this sandwich is a delightful combination of tastes and textures.

Two 12-oz. pork tenderloins
3 tbsp. German mustard, plus more for bread
Sea salt and freshly ground black pepper
German pretzel baguettes (allow 6 in. for
    each person)

1 cup ketchup
1 tbsp. curry powder
2 German garlic barrel pickles, sliced

Prepare grill to medium-high heat. Pat the tenderloins dry and rub with mustard. Sprinkle with salt and pepper and place on the grill. Grill for 10 minutes on each side, or until an instant-read thermometer inserted in the thickest part reads 155°F (68°C). Remove tenderloins from the grill and let stand, loosely covered with aluminum foil, for about 10 minutes (the internal temperature will rise by 5 to 10 degrees).

Slice the baguettes into 6-inch segments; slice open and spread with more mustard. Slice the cooked pork very thinly and divide among the prepared bread. Garnish with a mixture of the ketchup, curry powder, and sliced pickles, and serve.

Serves 4

black pepper chops with molasses butter

see variations page 142

These Southern-style chops are an all-American favorite.

1/4 cup sweet butter, softened
1 tbsp. molasses
1 tsp. fresh lemon juice

4 tbsp. coarsely ground black pepper
4 boneless center-loin pork chops,
      1 1/2 in. thick

In a small bowl blend the butter, molasses, and lemon juice with a fork. Cover the bowl and refrigerate until needed.

Rub the chops evenly on both sides with pepper. Grill the chops over a medium-hot grill for 12 to 15 minutes, turning once. To serve, top each pork chop with a tablespoon of the molasses butter.

Serves 4

st. louis pork steaks

see variations page 143

The seasoned cider vinegar leaves the pork chops juicy and unbelievably tasty, which perhaps explains why in St. Louis they pull out the grill to make this classic dish even in midwinter!

Five 1/2-in.-thick pork shoulder steaks
2 tbsp. seasoned salt, or to taste
1 tbsp. seasoned pepper, or to taste

2 cups apple cider vinegar
1 1/2 cups water
2 cups barbecue sauce

Season the pork steaks on both sides with seasoned salt and seasoned pepper. In a large bowl, stir together the vinegar and water, and season with seasoned salt and seasoned pepper to taste.

Preheat the grill to medium-low heat. Lightly oil the grill grate. Place the pork steaks on the grill. Baste the steaks with the vinegar mixture on both sides during the first 15 minutes of grilling. Continue to cook the steaks to desired doneness, allowing roughly 10 to 15 more minutes. Discard any remaining vinegar mixture at the end of cooking. At the end of the cooking process, brush liberally with barbecue sauce on both sides to glaze the steaks.

Serves 5

barbecued pork butt

see variations page 144

The triple flavoring element in this juicy pork—the rub, slather, and seasoning—makes for a satisfyingly layered flavor.

One 5 to 7-lb. pork butt
for Lola's mustard slather
1 cup spicy mustard
1/4 cup Worcestershire sauce
2 tbsp. fresh lemon juice
2 tsp. garlic powder
1 tsp. onion powder
1 tsp. fine ground black pepper
1/2 tsp. cayenne pepper
1/2 tsp. sea salt
for Kansas City Rib Doctor pork rub
1/4 cup granulated sugar

1/4 cup noniodized sea salt
1/8 cup brown sugar
4 tsp. chili powder
2 tsp. ground cumin
1 tsp. cayenne pepper
1 tsp. freshly ground black pepper
1 tsp. garlic powder
1 tsp. onion powder
for finishing pork
1/2 cup apple juice
1/2 cup barbecue sauce
2 tbsp. cider vinegar

Trim excess fat from the pork butt. To make the mustard slather, combine all the ingredients in a bowl and blend well. Cover and set aside. For the rub, combine all the ingredients and blend well. Set aside.

Using a pastry brush, cover the pork butt bottom, sides, and ends with the mustard slather. Season all over with the rub, reserving 1 tablespoon. Place on the grill fat-side up. Cook the butt for 8 hours. Baste every hour with apple juice. Turn the butt after 4 hours, and again

after 6 hours. If you are going to slice the butt, cook it to a temperature of 175°F to 185°F (80°C to 85°C). If you want to pull the pork, cook it to a higher temperature of 195°F to 205°F (90°C to 95°C).

If you're slicing the pork, slice and serve with sauce on the side. If pulling the pork, take two large or heavy-duty dinner forks and shred the pork, removing any fat. Add 1/2 cup barbecue sauce, 2 tablespoons cider vinegar, and 1 tablespoon rub, and blend well. Serve.

Serves 10–12

country-style pork ribs with southern barbecue sauce

see variations page 145

Ribs are one of the original finger foods, so don't be shy when eating with your hands. Just grab hold of a rib and take a big bite! Wash it down with some homemade lemonade.

for the rub
1/4 cup light brown sugar
2 tbsp. paprika
1 tbsp. granulated garlic
1 tbsp. chili powder
1 tbsp. onion powder
2 tsp. sea salt
2 tsp. coarse ground black pepper
1 tsp. oregano

4 lbs. country-style pork ribs
for the barbecue sauce
One 8-oz. can tomato sauce
1/3 cup molasses
1/4 cup vinegar
1 tsp. garlic powder
1 tsp. chili powder
1/2 tsp. ground black pepper
2 tsp. sea salt

Mix the brown sugar and all the dry spices to make the rub; coat the ribs with the rub on both sides. Set aside to rest. Meanwhile, in a small saucepan combine the tomato sauce, molasses, vinegar, garlic powder, chili powder, pepper, and salt. Simmer over medium heat for 15 minutes, stirring occasionally.

Preheat the grill to medium-hot. Grill ribs for about 20 to 30 minutes or until done, turning as needed to avoid flare-ups and burning. Glaze with the barbecue sauce, and continue to cook until sticky.

Serves 8

barbecued polish pork loin

see variations page 146

Any smoked sausage could be used here, but Polish varieties are especially good.

1 tbsp. sugar
1 tsp. paprika
1 tsp. seasoned salt
1 tsp. garlic salt
1 tsp. onion salt
1 tsp. celery salt
1 tsp. dry mustard

1 tsp. finely ground black pepper
3 to 5 lbs. boneless pork loin
One 6- to 8-in. cooked Polish or smoked
    sausage
1/4 cup canola oil
1 medium onion, sliced thin

Combine the rub ingredients (everything except the pork loin, sausage, oil, and onion), blend well, and set aside.

With a long, sharp, thin knife, cut a cross in the middle of the eye of the pork loin, all the way through, large enough to stuff the sausage through it. Push the sausage into the pork loin. (If the sausage isn't stiff enough to push, freeze it first.) Rub the stuffed pork loin with the oil and season it with the rub.

Place it in your smoker, top with the sliced onion, and cook at 230°F to 250°F (110°C to 120°C), covered, using the indirect method. The loin must reach an internal temperature of 155°F (68°C). Slice to serve.

Serves 10–12

lamb chops dijon

see variations page 147

A simple but vibrant French-style recipe that brings out the wonderful taste of good lamb chops.

12 small lamb loin chops
3 tbsp. grated orange zest
3 tbsp. chopped fresh thyme

2/3 cup Dijon mustard
2 tbsp. packed light brown sugar
Salt and pepper to taste

Trim any excess fat from the lamb chops. Mix the orange zest and thyme in a bowl. Add the mustard and brown sugar, and stir to combine. Preheat the grill.

Brush about half of the mixture onto each side of the chops and place on the hot grill for about 2 minutes per side. Turn the chops over and brush the other half of the mixture onto them. Continue until done. Season with salt and pepper, and serve.

Serves 4

tandoori rack of lamb

see variations page 148

The traditional Indian spice rub on this rack of lamb gives it a fantastic flavor. The lamb is seared hot to seal in the juices and give it a deliciously crusty surface.

1/2 tsp. ground turmeric	1 tsp. brown sugar
1/2 tsp. curry powder	1/4 tsp. dry mustard
1/2 tsp. ground cumin	1/4 tsp. ground ginger
1/2 tsp. ground coriander	One 8-bone rack of lamb

Combine the turmeric, curry powder, cumin, coriander, brown sugar, mustard, and ginger. Dry the rack of lamb with paper towels and coat it with the spice rub. Set aside for 1 hour.

Preheat the grill. Place the lamb on the hot grill and sear on each side for about 2 minutes. Reduce the heat or move the lamb to a cooler part of the grill and continue grilling until the internal temperature reaches about 130°F (54°C).

Allow to rest for about 10 minutes, then cut into chops and serve.

Serves 8

spicy rotisserie leg of lamb

see variations page 149

Here is another dish that draws on the aromatic flavors of Asia to make a delicately spiced joint of lamb.

One 4-lb. boneless leg of lamb, trimmed
3 tbsp. plain yogurt
2 tsp. ground turmeric
1 tsp. ground cardamom
1 tsp. grated fresh gingerroot

1 tsp. paprika
2 large cloves garlic, minced
1/2 tsp. salt (more if needed)
1/2 tsp. ground black pepper

Trim any extra fat from the lamb and make diagonal slits on both sides of the leg. Combine all the remaining ingredients in a small mixing bowl and spread over the lamb. Make sure the marinade is brushed into the diagonal slits. Reserve some marinade for basting. Cover the lamb and refrigerate for 1 hour.

Preheat the grill to low and skewer the lamb securely on a rotisserie rod. Cook on the grill for 1 1/2 to 2 hours. Baste with the reserved marinade every 15 minutes. When finished, remove the leg of lamb from the grill and let it rest for 10 minutes before slicing.

Serves 6

grilled denver lamb ribs

see variations page 150

Although lamb is growing in popularity, you may have difficulty finding whole breasts of lamb in your market. If so, you can ask your butcher for lamb riblets, which are the breasts already cut into individual pieces.

4 slabs lamb ribs
for the marinade
1/2 cup soy sauce
1/4 cup hoisin sauce
2 tbsp. white wine vinegar

2 tbsp. sweet Chinese rice wine
2 tbsp. clover honey
1 tsp. garlic powder
1 tsp. crushed red pepper flakes
1/4 cup pineapple juice

Trim extra fat from ribs. Mix all the marinade ingredients in a large container. Place the ribs in a resealable plastic bag, pour the marinade over the ribs, and marinate overnight. Remove the ribs from the marinade. Place the marinade in a small saucepan, bring to a boil, reduce the heat, and simmer for 5 minutes. Use the reserved marinade as a baste.

Preheat the grill to medium-high heat, brush with oil, and immediately place the ribs on the oiled grate. Cook until dark grill marks develop (about 3 minutes), basting as you cook, then turn and cook for another 2 to 3 minutes. Move the ribs to a cooler part of the grill, and cook until the ribs are medium-rare (about 4 to 8 minutes longer). Remove from the heat, cover, and rest for 5 minutes before serving as is, or with a sauce of your choice.

Serves 4

barbecued texas cabrito

see variations page 151

Cabrito is a delicacy with many ardent admirers, but you must use a young suckling kid, no more than 30 or 40 days old. The best time to get cabrito is May through October— after October you should be skeptical.

1 hind leg baby goat, trimmed
1/2 cup spicy mustard
for the rub
1/4 cup lemon pepper
1/4 cup chili powder
2 tbsp. garlic powder
1 tsp. cayenne pepper

for the cabrito mop
12 oz. beer
2 tbsp. Worcestershire sauce
2 tbsp. fresh lemon juice
1 tbsp. fresh lime juice
1 tbsp. chili powder
1/2 tsp. cayenne pepper

Rub the meat completely with the mustard. Add the rub spices to a 2-gallon resealable plastic bag, seal, and shake until mixed. Place the meat in the bag and coat with the rub. Refrigerate overnight. Before grilling, mix the ingredients for the mop.

Prepare the grill for the indirect heat method. Remove the meat from the bag and place on the grid. Smoke for 25 minutes at 250°F (120°C). Baste with the mop every 25 minutes. Smoke for 2 to 3 hours or until the internal temperature reaches 155°F to 165 (68°C to 75°C). Remove the meat from the grill, loosely cover with foil, and let it cool for 10 to 15 minutes before slicing. Serve with barbecue sauce on the side.

Serves 6–8

teriyaki pork burgers

see base recipe page 115

herbed pork burgers
Replace the soy sauce, orange juice, ginger, and sugar with 1/3 cup brandy; 1 tablespoon celery salt; 2 teaspoons each of dried sage and dried rosemary; 1 teaspoon freshly ground pepper; 1/2 teaspoon each of dried thyme and crumbled dried summer savory; 1/4 teaspoon freshly grated nutmeg; and 1 teaspoon oil. Proceed with base recipe.

new orleans andouille burgers
Replace the soy sauce, orange juice, ginger, and sugar with 2 tablespoons each of paprika, garlic powder, and freshly ground pepper; 1 tablespoon each of sea salt, cayenne pepper, onion powder, dried oregano, and dried thyme; 1 1/2 teaspoons each of chili powder and filé powder; and 1 teaspoon ground cumin. Proceed with base recipe.

brat burgers
Replace the soy sauce, orange juice, ginger, and sugar with 2 teaspoons each of salt, sugar, dry mustard, paprika, ground coriander, dried sage, and freshly ground pepper; and 1/4 teaspoon each of dried rosemary, grated nutmeg, and cayenne pepper. Proceed with base recipe.

italian burgers
Replace the soy sauce, orange juice, ginger, and sugar with 2 teaspoons garlic powder; 1 teaspoon each of crushed fennel seeds, ground coriander, dried parsley flakes, seasoned salt, and onion powder; 1/2 teaspoon black pepper; and 1/4 teaspoon cayenne pepper. Proceed with base recipe

variations

jerk barbecued ribs

see base recipe page 116

spice-rubbed ribs
Replace jerk marinade with a rub made from 1/4 cup light brown sugar; 1/4 cup seasoned salt; 1 teaspoon each of ground allspice, black pepper, ground cumin, and ground ginger; and 1/2 teaspoon ground cinnamon. Proceed with base recipe.

finger-lickin' ribs
Replace jerk marinade with a rub made from 1/2 cup cane sugar, 1/2 cup fine grind raw sugar, 2 tablespoons each of seasoned salt, garlic salt, fine ground black pepper, and paprika, 1 tablespoon each of Old Bay Seasoning, onion salt, and celery salt, and 1 teaspoon each of dry mustard, granulated onion, and ground basil. Proceed with base recipe.

zesty no-salt herbal ribs
Replace jerk marinade with a rub made from 1 cup granulated sugar; 1/2 cup light brown sugar; 1/4 cup chili powder; 3 tablespoons finely ground black pepper; 1 tablespoon each of chopped fresh dill, garlic powder, and onion powder; 2 teaspoons each of celery seeds, New Mexico chili powder, lemon juice powder; and 1 teaspoon each of dried basil, dried marjoram, dry mustard, cayenne, dried parsley, dried rosemary, and rubbed sage. Proceed with base recipe.

carolina-country barbecued ribs
Replace jerk marinade with a marinade made from 1 cup cider vinegar; 1 tablespoon each of red pepper flakes, minced garlic, and sugar; 1/2 cup water; 2 teaspoons dry mustard; and 1 teaspoon each of freshly ground black pepper and dried thyme. Proceed with base recipe.

german-style barbecued pork sandwich

see base recipe page 119

bourbon pork tenderloins
Omit the mustard rub. Marinate the pork for 2 hours in a mixture of 3/4 cup soy sauce; 1/2 cup bourbon; 1/4 cup each of Worcestershire sauce, water, and canola oil; 4 pressed garlic cloves; 3 tablespoons brown sugar; 2 tablespoons ground black pepper; 1 teaspoon salt; and 1/2 teaspoon ground ginger. Proceed with base recipe.

korean-style pork tenderloins
Omit the mustard rub. Marinate the pork for 2 hours in a mixture of 2 tablespoons sugar, 1/3 cup soy sauce, 3 tablespoons rice vinegar, 1 tablespoon each of grated gingerroot and sesame oil, 1/2 teaspoon crushed red pepper flakes, and 4 pressed garlic cloves. Proceed with base recipe.

pork tenderloins with chipotle maple sauce
Omit the mustard rub. Marinate the pork for 2 hours in a mixture of 2 teaspoons ground coriander, 1 teaspoon garlic powder, 1/2 teaspoon ground ginger, 1 tablespoon vegetable oil, salt and pepper to taste. Serve with a chipotle maple sauce: mix 2 tablespoons sherry vinegar, 1/4 cup maple syrup, and 2 teaspoons chipotle chili hot sauce. Proceed with base recipe.

thai tenderloins
Omit the mustard rub. Marinate the pork for 2 hours in a mixture of 1 teaspoon Louisiana hot sauce; 1/4 cup fresh orange juice; grated zest of 1 orange; 2 tablespoons fresh cilantro; 2 cloves garlic; 3 tablespoons brown sugar; 2 tablespoons each of fresh parsley, soy sauce, and peanut butter; 1 tablespoon grated fresh gingerroot; 1 teaspoon cayenne. Proceed with base recipe.

variations

black pepper chops with molasses butter

see base recipe page 120

chuletas de puerco criollas
Instead of the molasses butter, marinate chops for several hours in a mixture of: 6 large pressed cloves garlic; 1/4 teaspoon dried oregano; 1/4 teaspoon toasted ground cumin; 1/2 cup sour (Seville) orange juice; 2 large onions, thinly sliced; 1/4 cup olive oil; and 1/2 cup dry sherry. Remove chops and onions from marinade. Grill the onions alongside the chops.

iowa chops with blue cheese sauce
Instead of molasses butter, make a blue cheese sauce by stirring 2 tablespoons flour into 4 tablespoons melted sweet butter. Slowly pour in 1/4 cup milk and heat gently to thicken. Stir in 1 tablespoon chopped fresh parsley; 1 teaspoon garlic powder; 1 teaspoon sugar; 1 small tomato, peeled, seeded, and diced; and 1/2 cup crumbled blue cheese.

cherry pork chops
Instead of serving with molasses butter, make a rub from 1 tablespoon lemon pepper, 1 teaspoon chicken bouillon granules, and 1/4 teaspoon ground mace. Serve one heated 16-ounce can of cherry pie filling with the grilled chops.

grilled curry pork chops
Instead of serving with molasses butter, marinate the chops for 2 hours in a mixture of: 1/4 cup soy sauce and 1 tablespoon each of garlic powder, mild curry powder, crushed coriander seeds, cracked black pepper, and brown sugar. Grill as in the base recipe.

variations

st. louis pork steaks

see base recipe page 123

grilled pork steaks adobo
Omit the vinegar baste and barbecue sauce. Serve grilled pork with a sauce made by simmering in a saucepan for 10 minutes the following ingredients: one 8-ounce can tomato sauce; 1/4 cup packed light brown sugar; 2 tablespoons each of Worcestershire sauce, white wine vinegar, and canned adobo sauce; 2 canned chipotle peppers, seeded and chopped; 1 tablespoon onion powder; 1 tablespoon chili powder; and 1 teaspoon garlic salt.

tangy grilled pork steaks
Omit vinegar baste. Replace rub with a mixture of 2 tablespoons garlic salt, 1 tablespoon onion salt, and 1 tablespoon lemon pepper. For a sauce, stir together 1/4 cup ketchup, 1/4 cup Dijon mustard, 2 tablespoons mustard, and 2 teaspoons crushed red pepper flakes.

albuquerque-style pork steaks
Replace the rub and vinegar baste with a rub made from 6 tablespoons chili powder, 1 tablespoon sugar, 1 tablespoon onion powder, and 2 teaspoons each of ground cumin, garlic powder, dried oregano, and sea salt. Serve with a sauce made from 2 cups pico de gallo, 4 sliced avocados, and 2 tablespoons fresh lime juice.

grilled pork steaks with hoisin glaze
Omit the vinegar baste, rub, and barbecue sauce. Serve grilled pork with a sauce made by combining 1/2 cup hoisin sauce, 1 pressed clove garlic, 1 tablespoon each of cider vinegar and honey, 2 teaspoons grated gingerroot, and a sprinkling of crushed red pepper flakes.

variations

barbecued pork butt

see base recipe page 124

chuckwagon pork butt
Replace the Kansas City rub with one made from 1 tablespoon freshly ground black pepper;
2 teaspoons kosher salt or sea salt; 2 teaspoons chili powder; and 1 teaspoon each of sugar,
onion powder, garlic powder, dried parsley, and dried oregano.

southern barbecue pork butt
Replace the Kansas City rub with one made from 3 tablespoons dried oregano and
2 tablespoons each of garlic powder, freshly ground black pepper, hot chili powder, and salt.

brown sugar pork butt
Replace the Kansas City rub with one made from 1/4 cup brown sugar; 1 tablespoon each of
garlic salt, coarse ground black pepper, paprika, and chili powder, 1 teaspoon celery salt;
1/4 teaspoon ground allspice; and 1/4 teaspoon ground thyme.

spicy southeast pork butt
Replace the Kansas City rub with one made from 2 tablespoons chili powder; 1 tablespoon
each of paprika, hot paprika, dried oregano, cayenne pepper, garlic powder, and sea salt; and
2 teaspoons each of ground cumin, crushed red pepper flakes, and coarse ground black pepper.

variations

country-style pork ribs with southern barbecue sauce

see base recipe page 127

chipotle country ribs

Instead of the rub and sauce, marinate the ribs for several hours in the following mixture, pureed in a blender: 1/2 cup red wine vinegar; 1 cup olive oil; a 7-ounce can chipotle chilies in adobo sauce; 4 scallions, chopped; 1 jalapeño, seeds and stems removed; 3 tablespoons fresh oregano; 3 cloves garlic, chopped; 1/2 tablespoon salt; and black pepper to taste.

buzz's country ribs

Instead of the rub, marinate ribs in the following mixture: 2 tablespoons onion powder; 1 tablespoon each of sea salt, coarse ground black pepper, and garlic powder; 2 cups each of apple cider vinegar and apple cider; 1 cup packed light brown sugar; 1/4 cup Worcestershire sauce; and 2 tablespoons crushed red pepper flakes. Serve with 2 cups barbecue sauce.

char siu chinese barbecued pork

Instead of the rub and sauce, make a glaze by mixing together 1/4 cup hoisin sauce; 2 tablespoons each chicken stock, Chinese rice wine, and dark soy sauce; 1 pressed clove garlic; 1 1/2 tablespoons honey; 3/4 teaspoon sea salt; and a few drops of red food coloring.

country ribs with peach jalapeño glaze

Instead of the rub and sauce, make a glaze by mixing together 3 tablespoons peach jelly, 3 tablespoons corn syrup, 1 tablespoon ketchup, 2 minced and seeded jalapeños, and 1 teaspoon ground cumin. Simmer together for 15 minutes and brush over the pork ribs while grilling.

variations

barbecued polish pork loin

see base recipe page 128

tex-mex country pork loin

Omit the sausage and replace the rub with: 2 tablespoons light brown sugar; 1 tablespoon garlic; 2 teaspoons each of ground cumin, chili powder, onion powder, fine grind black pepper, and paprika; and 1 teaspoon jalapeño powder. Proceed with base recipe.

bacon-wrapped barbecued pork loin

Omit the sausage and wrap the loin with: 1/2 pound sliced bacon. Replace the rub with: 1 cup dark brown sugar; 1/4 cup paprika; 2 tablespoons seasoned salt; 1 tablespoon each of black pepper, white pepper, cayenne pepper, garlic salt, onion salt, and dry mustard; and 2 teaspoons rubbed sage. Proceed with base recipe.

gourmet pepper-crusted barbecued pork loin

Omit the sausage and replace the rub with: 1/4 cup coarse-ground gourmet peppercorns; 1/4 cup light brown sugar; 2 tablespoons each of dry mustard, celery salt, and garlic salt; and 1 teaspoon chipotle powder. Proceed with base recipe.

elegant barbecued pork loin

Omit everything except the pork loin. Paint the pork loin with 1/2 cup balsamic vinegar. Combine 2 tablespoons each of garlic salt and coarse ground black pepper and 1 tablespoon crushed rosemary leaves. Sprinkle this over the loin before cooking. Proceed with base recipe.

variations

lamb chops dijon

see base recipe page 131

armenian lamb chops
Replace the mustard glaze with a marinade: 1 minced onion, 1/2 cup red wine, 1/4 cup chopped Armenian parsley, 2 teaspoons each minced fresh mint, and minced fresh basil. Marinate chops for 2 hours. Proceed with base recipe.

grilled ginger and red wine lamb chops
Replace the mustard glaze with a marinade: 3 tablespoons olive oil; 2 tablespoons each of red wine and soy sauce; 2 cloves pressed garlic; 1 tablespoon each lemon juice and grated fresh ginger; 1 1/2 teaspoons onion powder; 1/4 teaspoon cayenne pepper, and 3–4 tablespoons lukewarm water. Marinate chops for 2 hours. Proceed with base recipe.

apple-glazed lamb chops
Replace the mustard glaze with an apple glaze: heat 1/2 cup apple jelly, 1/4 cup lemon juice concentrate, and 1/4 cup steak sauce gently in a saucepan. Add salt and pepper to taste, and glaze the chops before grilling as directed. Proceed with base recipe.

chili-rubbed lamb chops
Replace mustard glaze with a chili rub: 1 1/2 tablespoons chili powder; 2 teaspoons ground cumin; 1 teaspoon each of dried thyme, sugar, and black pepper; 3/4 teaspoon salt, and 1/4 teaspoon ground allspice. Serve with 2 cups hot pepper jelly on the side. Proceed with base recipe.

variations

tandoori rack of lamb

see base recipe page 132

arizona rack of lamb
Replace spice rub with: 8 tablespoons unsalted butter, softened; 2 teaspoons each of chili powder and paprika; 1 teaspoon ground cumin and garlic powder; 1/2 teaspoon each of onion powder, chipotle powder, oregano, and freshly ground black pepper. Proceed with base recipe.

curried rack of lamb
Replace spice rub with: 2 tablespoons sea salt; 1 tablespoon curry powder; 2 teaspoons onion powder, 1 teaspoon each of freshly ground black pepper, garlic powder, and jalapeño powder; 1/2 teaspoon ground allspice. Proceed with base recipe.

marinated rack of lamb with orange marmalade glaze
Omit spice rub. Combine 1 cup olive oil; 2 tablespoons garlic salt; 1 teaspoon each of crushed dried thyme leaves, crushed dried rosemary leaves, and coarse ground black pepper. Marinate lamb for 2 hours. Combine 1 cup orange marmalade, 1/2 cup fresh orange juice, 2 tablespoons fresh lemon juice, 1 tablespoon triple sec, and 1/8 teaspoon each of sea salt and white pepper. Puree. Heat in a saucepan, adding 2 tablespoons unsalted butter. Use this mixture to glaze the marinated lamb as it cooks.

honey glazed rack of lamb
Replace spice rub with 2 tablespoons lemon pepper and 1 tablespoon garlic salt. Combine in a small bowl 3 tablespoons each of honey, fresh lemon juice, and soy sauce; and 2 cloves garlic, pressed. Use this mixture to glaze the lamb as it cooks.

variations

spicy rotisserie leg of lamb

see base recipe page 135

garlic-dijon leg of lamb
Omit everything except the lamb. Combine 1/2 cup Dijon mustard; 4 large cloves garlic, each sliced into 4 thin slivers; 2 tablespoons onion salt; 1 tablespoon coarse ground black pepper. Proceed with base recipe.

balsamic vinegar and rosemary leg of lamb
Omit everything except the lamb. Mix 1/4 cup balsamic vinegar, 2 tablespoons clover honey, 2 teaspoons each of olive oil, crushed dried rosemary leaves, and garlic powder; and 1 teaspoon each of sea salt and freshly ground black pepper. Proceed with base recipe.

greek-flavored leg of lamb
Omit everything except the lamb. Mix 1/4 cup Worcestershire sauce; 2 teaspoons dried oregano; 1 1/2 teaspoons onion powder; 1 1/2 teaspoons garlic powder; 1 teaspoon each of sea salt, freshly ground black pepper, pulverized beef-flavored bouillon granules, and dried parsley flakes; and 1/2 teaspoon ground cinnamon and ground nutmeg. Proceed with base recipe.

classic leg of lamb
Omit everything except the lamb. Mix 1/4 cup extra-virgin olive oil; 2 tablespoons kosher salt; and 1 tablespoon each of coarse ground black pepper, dried minced garlic, and crushed dried rosemary leaves. Proceed with base recipe.

variations

grilled denver lamb ribs

see base recipe page 136

lamb ribs provençal
Replace marinade with: 1 tablespoon dried parsley; 2 teaspoons each of garlic powder, onion salt, and *herbes de Provence*, and 1 teaspoon each of freshly ground black pepper, kosher salt, and olive oil. Proceed with base recipe.

spiced lamb riblets
Replace marinade with: 1 cup plain low-fat yogurt, 2 tablespoons spicy mustard, 2 large pressed cloves garlic, 1 tablespoon each of soy sauce and fresh lemon juice, and 1 teaspoon cayenne. Proceed with base recipe.

barbecued lamb ribs
Replace marinade with: 2 cups barbecue sauce; 1/2 cup white wine; 2 tablespoons oil; 1 tablespoon sugar; 1 lemon, sliced thinly; 1/2 teaspoon each of crushed peppercorns, fresh thyme leaves, and crushed juniper berries; 1 teaspoon salt. Proceed with base recipe.

spicy barbecue colorado lamb ribs
Replace marinade with: 1/2 cup apple cider; 1 tablespoon grated fresh ginger; 2 tablespoons each of cider vinegar, canola oil, soy sauce, and clover honey; and 1 clove garlic, pressed. Make a spicy barbecue sauce to serve with the ribs by combining in a saucepan: 1 cup each of tomato paste and cider vinegar, 1/2 cup each of molasses and packed brown sugar, 1/4 cup each of soy sauce and Worcestershire sauce, 2 tablespoons yellow mustard, 1 teaspoon each of sea salt and black pepper, and 1/2 teaspoon cayenne. Proceed with base recipe.

barbecued texas cabrito

see base recipe page 138

jerked cabrito
Replace rub with a mixture of: 1 cup grated onion; 1/2 cup soy sauce; 6 large pressed cloves garlic; 1 tablespoon each of minced fresh thyme leaves, ground allspice, and sea salt; 2 teaspoons freshly ground black pepper; 1 teaspoon ground cinnamon; 1/2 teaspoon ground nutmeg; and 1 habañero chili. Reduce mop ingredients to: one 12-ounce can beer and 1/4 cup fresh lemon juice. Proceed with base recipe.

kansas city cabrito
Replace rub with a mixture of: 2 tablespoons sea salt and 1 tablespoon each of coarse ground black pepper, garlic powder, onion powder, ground cumin, and cayenne. Reduce mop ingredients to: one 12-ounce can beer and 1/4 cup fresh lemon juice. Proceed with base recipe.

barbecued cabrito
Replace rub with a mixture of 3 tablespoons salt and pepper, and 1 tablespoon paprika. Alter mop recipe to: 5 pressed cloves garlic, 4 cups each of vegetable oil and cider vinegar, 2 cups water, 1 cup Worcestershire sauce, 2 bay leaves, and 2 halved and juiced lemons. Proceed with base recipe.

cooper's cabrito
Replace rub with a mixture of 3 tablespoons coarse ground black pepper, 2 tablespoons kosher salt, and 2 teaspoons cayenne pepper. Proceed with base recipe.

succulent beef

Nothing brings out the natural flavors of beef better than the grill. Whether you're in the mood for a simple steak or want to go all out with a succulent prime rib, there's something here to satisfy your beef craving.

beef brisket with spicy rub

see variations page 180

Served with an angel's mustard slather, this is melt-in-the-mouth tender and tasty.

2 tsp. garlic powder
1 tsp. onion powder
1/2 tsp. cayenne pepper
1 tsp. fine grind black pepper
1/2 tsp. white pepper
1/2 tsp. sea salt
2 tbsp. soy sauce
2 tbsp. white wine
2 tbsp. Worcestershire sauce
1 cup Dijon or yellow mustard
1 cup granulated sugar

1 tbsp. seasoned salt
1 tbsp. garlic salt
1 tbsp. onion salt
1 tbsp. celery salt
2 tbsp. paprika
1 tbsp. chili powder
1 tsp. ground ginger
1 tsp. chipotle powder
1/2 tsp. ground allspice
1/2 tsp. ground dry mustard
One 4- to 8-lb. brisket

To make the mustard slather, put the garlic powder, onion powder, cayenne, peppers, and salt in a bowl. Blend in the soy sauce, white wine, and Worcestershire sauce, and stir with a whisk to dissolve the spices. Stir in the mustard and incorporate all the ingredients. Cover and set aside. Combine all the dry seasonings and blend well to make a rub. Set aside. Trim most of the fat from the brisket, leaving 1/4 to 1/8-inch fat cap. Using a pastry brush, cover the lean side of the brisket with the mustard slather. Sprinkle on the rub. Turn the brisket over and repeat the process on the fat side. Don't forget to season the ends and sides. Place the brisket on your grill and smoke for 8 to 12 hours or until a skewer inserted in the flat part of the brisket, against the grain, goes in and comes out with no resistance.

Serves 8

carne asada

see variations page 181

This Mexican classic is perfect for outdoor eating on lazy summer evenings.

1/2 cup tequila
1/4 cup fresh lime juice
1/4 cup fresh lemon juice
1/4 cup fresh orange juice
4 cloves garlic, pressed
1/2 cup grated onion
Tabasco sauce to taste

1 tsp. freshly ground black pepper
2 lbs. flank or skirt steak
12 flour tortillas
1 cup salsa
1 cup guacamole
Tabasco or taco sauce to taste

Mix tequila, juices, garlic, onion, Tabasco, and pepper in a bowl. Reserve 1/4 cup of the marinade. Add the meat to the remaining marinade, cover the bowl, and marinate for 4 hours or (for better results) overnight. Turn occasionally while marinating.

Preheat a grill to medium. Place a few drops of water on each tortilla, stack, and wrap in heavy-duty aluminum foil. Place on the grill. Remove the meat from the bowl and discard the marinade. Place the steak on the grill. Turn the meat and tortillas once during cooking, and brush the steak with the reserved 1/4 cup marinade. Cook to your liking (12 to 15 minutes for medium-rare for the flank steak, less for the skirt steaks). Cut into thin slices across the grain. Place a few slices of steak on each tortilla with salsa and guacamole, and serve with Tabasco or taco sauce.

Serves 6

pale ale porterhouse

see variations page 182

Porterhouse steaks contain a large proportion of tenderloin, making them especially tasty and tender.

Two 1 1/2-in. porterhouse steaks, 2 lbs. each
1 tbsp. kosher or other coarse salt
1 tbsp. coarse ground black pepper

2 tbsp. unsalted butter
1 cup flat pale ale at room temperature
2 tbsp. Worcestershire sauce

Generously sprinkle the steaks with salt and pepper, and let them sit, covered, at room temperature for 30 to 45 minutes. Melt the butter in a small saucepan over medium heat. Remove the pan from the heat, stir in the ale and Worcestershire sauce, and reserve the mixture. Prepare the grill for a two-level fire capable of cooking first on high heat and then on medium heat.

Keeping the smaller, more tender sections angled away from the hottest part of the grill, grill the steaks, uncovered, for 2 1/2 to 3 minutes per side. Move the steaks to medium heat, turning them again, and continue grilling for 3 to 4 minutes per side for medium-rare doneness. Steaks should be turned a minimum of three times (more often if juice begins to form on surface). If grilling covered, sear both sides of the meat first on high heat, uncovered, for 2 1/2 to 3 minutes; finish cooking, covered, over medium heat for 5 to 7 minutes, turning the steaks once midway.

Transfer the steaks to a platter and immediately top with equal amounts of beer-butter mixture. At the table, slice the steaks from the bones in thin strips and serve hot, making sure to spoon meat juices, beer, and butter on each portion.

Serves 4-6

the ultimate steakhouse burger

see variations page 183

A classic burger, stripped back to its basics and unadulterated by extra flavorings.

8 slices bacon
1 cup fresh Italian bread cubes without cruse or
sesame seeds
1/4 cup whole milk
1 1/2 lbs. lean ground beef (or ground chuck)

1 tsp. sea salt
1 tsp. freshly ground black pepper or to taste
2 large cloves garlic, pressed
Garnish: sliced tomatoes, onions, lettuce leaves

Fry the bacon in a large skillet over medium heat until crisp. Drain on paper towels. Spoon 3 tablespoons bacon fat into a heatproof bowl and refrigerate while preparing the other ingredients. Place the bread into a small bowl, add milk, and let the mixture sit until saturated, about 5 minutes. Using a fork, mash the bread and milk into a smooth paste. Break the beef into small pieces in a medium bowl, then add the salt and pepper with the garlic, bread paste, and reserved bacon fat. With your hands, lightly knead together so the mixture forms a cohesive mass.

Divide the meat mixture into 4 equal patties about 3/4-inch thick. Grill over high heat on a preheated grill for that charred flavor, until both sides are seared. Allow 4 to 5 minutes per side for medium rare, or longer if desired. Do not press down on the burgers as they cook. Serve with bacon, sliced tomatoes, onions, lettuce leaves or any other garnish you choose. Use the lean beef if you use the bacon fat; otherwise, use ground chuck.

Serves 4

beer-marinated peppered t-bones

see variations page 184

Marinating in beer tenderizes the steaks as well as flavoring them.

1 cup grated onion
3/4 cup flat beer
3/4 cup bottled chili sauce
2 tbsp. chopped fresh parsley
3 tbsp. Dijon-style mustard
1 tbsp. Worcestershire sauce
1 tbsp. light brown sugar

1 tsp. paprika
1/2 tsp. freshly ground black pepper
Four 12- to 16-oz. T-bone steaks
1 tbsp. kosher salt or to taste
1 tbsp. cracked black pepper or to taste
Fresh herbs (optional)

In a small bowl combine onion, beer, chili sauce, parsley, mustard, Worcestershire sauce, brown sugar, paprika, and the 1/2 teaspoon pepper. Place steaks in marinade. Cover and refrigerate 4 to 6 hours or overnight, turning steaks over occasionally.

Remove steaks from marinade; discard marinade. Sprinkle both sides of steaks with kosher salt and the cracked black pepper.

Grill steaks on an uncovered grill directly over medium heat for 5 to 7 minutes. Turn and grill to desired doneness, allowing 7 to 10 minutes more for medium-rare doneness. If desired, garnish with minced fresh herbs.

Serves 4

grilled marinated sirloin steak

see variations page 185

The simple flavors of this marinade do not interfere with the fine taste of the steak.

One 1/2-lb. boneless beef top sirloin steak, cut
   1 in. thick and well trimmed
1/4 cup balsamic vinegar
2 tbsp. tomato paste
2 large cloves garlic, pressed

1 tbsp. fresh thyme leaves
1 tbsp. fresh marjoram leaves
1 tbsp. kosher salt or to taste
1 tsp. freshly ground black pepper

Place the steak in a shallow glass dish or pie pan. Combine the remaining ingredients; spread evenly over both sides of the steak. Let stand at room temperature for 30 minutes, or cover and refrigerate for up to 8 hours. Remove the steak from its marinade; discard the marinade.

Preheat a grill to medium. Grill the steak 4 to 5 inches from the heat source, 4 minutes per side for medium-rare, or to desired doneness.

Slice the steak into thin strips and serve immediately.

Serves 4

balsamic hanger steaks

see variations page 186

Cook hanger steaks quickly and serve them rare or medium-rare to prevent them from becoming tough. They are always best if they are on the rare side.

2 1/2 cups balsamic vinegar
1/2 cup Worcestershire sauce
1 1/3 cups brown sugar
1 tbsp. salt
Four 6 to 8-oz. hanger steaks
Salt and pepper to taste

Combine 2 cups of balsamic vinegar with Worcestershire sauce, brown sugar, and 1 tablespoon salt. Mix until the sugar is dissolved. Place hanger steaks in a resealable gallon-size plastic bag. Pour marinade over steaks, seal bag, and turn to coat. Marinate the steaks for 3 to 4 hours. Meanwhile place the remaining 1/2 cup of balsamic vinegar in a saucepan. Bring to a boil and reduce by half. Set aside and allow to cool. It will continue to thicken as it cools.

Remove the steaks from their marinade and discard the marinade. Season with salt and pepper. Place on a grill preheated to high. Grill for about 3 minutes per side, brushing each side with the thickened balsamic vinegar regularly while cooking. Grill until rare or medium-rare, remove from the grill, and serve. Cut each steak on the bias into thin slices. Fan the slices out on warm dinner plates.

Serves 4

tenderloin with herbed cheese

see variations page 187

Tenderloin is an excellent cut because it is taken from a part of the animal that does very little work—meaning that it will remain meltingly tender when grilled.

2 tbsp. softened cream cheese
2 tbsp. blue cheese, crumbled
1 tbsp. plain yogurt
1 tbsp. grated onion
2 tsp. freshly ground black pepper
Four 8-oz. beef tenderloin steaks

1 large garlic clove, halved
Cooking spray
1 tsp. sea salt or to taste
1 tsp. freshly ground black pepper
2 tsp. fresh chopped parsley

Combine the cream cheese, blue cheese, yogurt, onion, and pepper; reserve. Rub each side of the beef steaks with the garlic. Spray the steaks with cooking spray and season all over with salt and pepper to taste.

Grill the steaks for 5 to 6 minutes on a grill preheated to medium. Turn, and grill for 3 to 4 minutes more. Top each steak with an equal amount of the cheese mixture. Grill for an additional 1 to 2 minutes. Garnish with parsley and serve hot.

Serves 4

grilled flank steak with aïoli

see variations page 188

Aïoli, a rich and flavorsome garlic mayonnaise from Provence, is the perfect partner for steak.

1 1/2 lb. flank steak, trimmed of any sinew
1/2 cup red wine vinegar
2 cloves garlic, pressed
2 tbsp. olive oil
Cooking spray

for the aïoli
7 large cloves garlic
2 large egg yolks
2 tbsp. sherry vinegar
1/2 cup good-quality olive oil
Sea salt and freshly ground black pepper

Place the flank steak in a resealable plastic bag with the vinegar, garlic, and oil; shake to coat thoroughly. Marinate in the refrigerator for 4 to 8 hours or overnight.

Place the garlic and egg yolks in a blender or food processor, and pulse until the garlic is finely chopped. Add the vinegar and blend. With the blender or food processor running, slowly add the olive oil in a thin stream until the mixture thickens. Remove to a bowl and season to taste. Immediately refrigerate until ready for use.

Preheat grill. Remove the steak from the marinade and discard the marinade. Spray the steak with cooking spray and grill over medium heat for about 4 to 6 minutes on each side or until medium-rare. Remove from the grill and allow to rest for about 5 minutes. Slice the meat across the grain and serve at once with the aïoli on the side in small ramekins.

Serves 4

béarnaise butter

see variations page 189

This is the classic French accompaniment for a simply grilled steak.

3 shallots, minced
1/4 cup wine vinegar
1/4 cup white wine
1 tsp. dried tarragon
16 tablespoons unsalted butter, softened

1/2 tsp. sea salt
1 tsp. parsley flakes

In a small pan, combine the shallots, wine vinegar, wine, and tarragon. Bring to a boil and reduce to a thick glaze. Cool. Add this to the butter, and season with the parsley and salt, blending until incorporated. Place the butter mixture in the middle of a sheet of plastic wrap and form into a cylinder. Chill or freeze.

Slice off pieces just prior to taking the steak off the grill. Place them on the steak during the resting period, and they will melt beautifully over the top of the steak. Depending on how big your roll is, 1/4-inch-thick slices are usually appropriate.

Serves 4

strip steak simple

see variations page 190

The simplest seasonings are often the best, allowing the flavors of top-quality meat to speak for themselves.

4 strip steaks, 1 in. thick
1 tbsp. kosher salt
1 tbsp. freshly ground black pepper

Season the steaks all over with the salt and pepper to taste. Let the steaks rest, covered, for 30 minutes at room temperature.

Grill over high heat on a preheated grill for 8 to 10 minutes per side for medium-rare, or longer if desired. Rotate the steaks a quarter turn after the first 2 1/2 minutes on the grill to create crisscrossed grill marks. Remove from the grill, loosely cover with aluminum foil, and let rest for about 10 minutes.

Serves 4

barbecued baby beef ribs

see variations page 191

Grilling baby beef ribs is a traditional, delicious Korean technique. The ingredients for this rub and sauce are often readily on hand, making the dish a reliable standby.

for the dry rub
2 tbsp. freshly ground black pepper
1 tbsp. garlic salt
1 tbsp. onion salt
1 tbsp. sweet paprika
1 tsp. cayenne pepper or to taste
1 slab baby beef ribs

for the mopping sauce
1/4 cup canola oil
1/4 cup fresh lemon juice
2 tbsp. ketchup
1 tsp. freshly ground black pepper
1 tsp. dry mustard

Combine the dry rub ingredients and blend well. Season the ribs on both sides with the rub. Combine all the ingredients in the small saucepan for the mopping sauce. Heat for 10 minutes over medium or low heat.

Cook ribs using the indirect method between 230°F and 250°F (110°C and 120°C) for about 4 to 6 hours, depending on the size of the ribs. Turn the ribs after cooking 2 hours and brush with a light coat of the mopping sauce. Cook until the ribs are tender, mopping them occasionally. The ribs are done when they are pierced easily with a knife.

Serves 4

deviled chuck steak

see variations page 192

Chuck steak needs slow and careful cooking, but the overnight marinating involved here will help to tenderize it beautifully.

Two 3/4-in. boneless beef chuck blade steaks
Unseasoned meat tenderizer
1 cup beef stock
1/4 cup packed light brown sugar
1/4 cup fresh lemon juice
2 tbsp. Worcestershire sauce

2 tbsp. yellow mustard
1 tsp. garlic powder
1 tsp. freshly ground black pepper
1/2 tsp. curry powder
1/2 tsp. cayenne pepper
1/4 tsp. ground bay leaf

Trim any excess fat from the chuck steaks. Prepare the steak with meat tenderizer as the packet label directs, cover, and place in the refrigerator for about an hour.

Mix the rest of the ingredients in a bowl; set aside. Place the steaks in a 2-gallon resealable plastic bag and pour 3/4 of the marinade over. Seal and marinate for 4 to 6 hours or overnight in the refrigerator.

Place the steak on a preheated grill over medium heat; grill for 35 minutes for rare or until desired doneness, turning steak occasionally. Baste regularly with the reserved 1/4 of the marinade. Remove the steak from the grill. Set aside and cover loosely with aluminum foil for 5 to 10 minutes.

Serves 4-6

argentinian-style rib eye steaks

see variations page 193

No one cooks beef as well as the Argentinians, and this method is particularly successful.

4 rib eye steaks cut 1 in. thick
1 tsp. sea salt or to taste
1 tsp. freshly ground black pepper or to taste
3 tbsp. olive oil
3 tbsp. chopped fresh flat-leaf parsley

1 tbsp. chopped fresh oregano
3 or 4 cloves garlic, minced
1 tsp. cayenne pepper

Season the steaks all over with salt and pepper to taste. Grill the steaks on an uncovered grill directly over medium heat to desired doneness, turning once. Allow 8 to 10 minutes for medium-rare doneness or 12 to 15 minutes for medium doneness.

Meanwhile, for the sauce, stir together the olive oil, parsley, oregano, garlic, salt, and cayenne pepper. Spoon the sauce on top of the steaks for the last 2 minutes of grilling.

Serves 4

grilled chilean skirt steak

see variations page 194

Skirt steak is a tasty cut, and the haunting flavor of this Chilean rub makes it even more appetizing.

2 lbs. skirt steak
1 cup fresh lime juice (about 8 limes)
for the rub
2 tbsp. ground toasted cumin
1 tbsp. garlic powder
1/4 cup dried cilantro leaves, crushed
Kosher salt and freshly ground black pepper to
    taste

for the relish
1/2 cup finely chopped pitted green olives
1 tsp. crushed red pepper flakes, or to taste
1/4 cup olive oil
2 tbsp. freshly ground black pepper

Place the steak in a resealable plastic bag or shallow dish and pour the lime juice over it. Seal the bag or cover the dish the dish and let it sit in the refrigerator for 30 minutes to 1 hour, turning occasionally. In a small bowl, combine all the rub ingredients and mix well. Remove the steak from the marinade, pat dry with paper towels, and rub it all over with the spice rub, pressing gently to be sure it adheres. Grill over medium heat for 4 to 5 minutes per side for medium-rare.

Remove the steak from the heat, cover it loosely with foil, and allow it to rest for 5 minutes while you make the relish. In a medium bowl, combine all the relish ingredients and mix well. Slice the steak as thin as possible against the grain on a bias. Serve with the relish, warm flour tortillas, rice, and beans.

Serves 6

grilled veal chops with rosemary

see variations page 195

Veal cooked with wine and rosemary unites some of the classic flavors of Tuscany — and the aroma while it grills is sensational.

1/2 cup olive oil
1/4 cup dry red wine
1 1/2 tbsp. chopped fresh rosemary
4 large garlic cloves, pressed
1/2 tsp. sea salt
1/2 tsp. freshly ground black pepper
Six 8-oz. veal rib chops (3/4 to 1 in. thick)
Fresh rosemary sprigs

Whisk the oil, wine, rosemary, garlic, salt, and pepper to blend in a glass baking dish. Add the veal chops to the dish and turn to coat with the marinade. Let stand at room temperature for 1 hour or refrigerate for up to 4 hours, turning the veal occasionally.

Preheat a grill to medium. Remove the veal from its marinade, shaking off the excess. Season the veal chops with salt and pepper. Grill the veal to your desired doneness, allowing about 4 minutes per side for medium-rare. Transfer to a platter. Garnish with fresh rosemary sprigs and serve.

Serves 6

barbecued short ribs

see variations page 196

The rub used for cooking these short ribs is mouthwateringly savory—you'll want to eat them all.

3 tbsp. kosher salt
1/4 tsp. cayenne pepper
1/2 tsp. black pepper
1/2 tsp. garlic powder
1/2 tsp. onion powder

1/2 tsp. paprika
1/2 tsp. ground cumin
4 lbs. beef short ribs
Prepared barbecue sauce for basting

Combine all the ingredients except the ribs and barbecue sauce in a small bowl, mixing well. Remove what you need and store the remainder. Wash the ribs and pat them dry. Rub with seasoning mixture. Place a disposable drip pan under the grates of the barbecue and wipe the grates with oil to prevent sticking. Heat the grill to high. Place the ribs over the drip pan, cover, and reduce the heat to low. Baste the ribs at the end of the cooking process with the sauce of your choice. Baste once 20 minutes before ribs are done, and a second time 10 minutes later.

Average-sized ribs are cooked rare in 25–30 minutes, medium-rare in 35–40 minutes, and well done in 45–50 minutes. These times will vary according to the grill used and the size of the ribs. Small ribs may require less cooking time, while large ribs may need a little more time on the grill. Adjust accordingly.

Serves 4

grilled tri-tip roast

see variations page 197

Tri-tip is becoming increasingly popular because of its full flavor and lack of fat. Try preparing it with this basic rub for a sensational yet simple grilled feast.

1 tbsp. garlic powder
1 tbsp. onion powder
1 tbsp. paprika
1 tbsp. coarse ground black pepper
1 tbsp. kosher salt
3 to 4 lbs. tri-tip roast

Combine all the ingredients except the tri-tip and blend well. Lightly oil the cooking grate on your grill. Preheat the grill and prepare for indirect grilling or direct grilling. Combine the garlic powder, onion powder, paprika, pepper, and salt. Rub it over the surface of the tri-tip roast. Place the tri-tip on the grill, fat side up. You could place a drip pan under it to catch the juices, which will make a great gravy later.

With the grill on low, cook for about 4 hours or until the internal temperature reaches 145°F (63°C) for medium-rare, or up to 165°F (75°C) for medium-well. If you are going to grill directly, cook, covered, over medium heat, turning every 15 to 20 minutes, until reaching your desired temperature.

Serves 4

variations

beef brisket with spicy rub

see base recipe page 153

jack's brisket rub
Replace the spicy rub with a rub made from 1/4 cup salt; 2 tablespoons each of white and brown sugar; 2 teaspoons each of dry mustard, onion powder, garlic powder, and dried basil; 1 teaspoon black pepper; 3/4 teaspoon dried coriander; 1/2 teaspoon dried savory; and 1/2 teaspoon ground cumin. Proceed with basic recipe.

texas brisket rub
Replace the spicy rub with a rub made from 1/4 cup coarse ground black pepper, 3 tablespoons kosher salt, 2 tablespoons paprika, and 1 tablespoon cayenne. Proceed with basic recipe.

spicy kansas city brisket rub
Replace the spicy rub with a rub made from 4 tablespoons paprika; 2 tablespoons chili powder; 1 tablespoon each of ground black pepper, ground white pepper, white sugar, ground cumin, garlic powder, light brown sugar, dried oregano, and celery salt; 2 teaspoons cayenne pepper; and 1 teaspoon dry mustard. Proceed with basic recipe.

stu carpenter's brisket rub
Replace the spicy rub with a rub made from 2 tablespoons each of black pepper, brown sugar, and paprika; 1 tablespoon sea salt; 2 teaspoons garlic powder; 1 teaspoon each of chili powder, onion powder, ground cumin, and white sugar; and 1/2 teaspoon each of dry mustard and chipotle powder. Proceed with basic recipe.

carne asada

see base recipe page 154

manuel's fajitas
Replace the marinade with one made by combining 1/2 cup soy sauce, 1/2 cup fresh lemon juice, 1 cup packed light brown sugar, and 1 tablespoon each of onion powder, garlic powder, and ground ginger. Wrap slices of grilled meat inside each tortilla.

west texas grilled fajitas
Replace the marinade with one made by combining 1/2 cup fresh lime juice; 1/4 cup red wine vinegar; 2 tablespoons each of soy sauce, chili powder, ground cumin, light molasses, and chopped cilantro; 4 large cloves garlic, pressed; and 1 teaspoon ground pepper. Wrap slices of grilled meat inside each tortilla.

bichelmeyer's meat market fajitas
Replace the marinade with one made by combining 4 large cloves garlic, pressed; 1 jalapeño chili pepper, seeded and minced; 1/2 cup canola oil; 1/4 cup each of fresh lime juice and cider vinegar; and 1 tablespoon sugar. Wrap slices of grilled meat inside each tortilla.

spiky lime carne asada
Replace the marinade with one made by combining 1 cup lime juice, 1/2 cup olive oil, and 1/2 cup loosely packed chopped cilantro leaves and stalks. Wrap slices of grilled meat inside each tortilla

variations

pale ale porterhouse

see base recipe page 157

porterhouse steaks with mushroom and garlic sauce
Replace the beer-butter mixture with a mushroom and garlic sauce. Make this by sautéing in a skillet 1 pound sliced mushrooms, 3 pressed large cloves garlic, and 1 tablespoon canola oil until the mushrooms are soft. Whisk in 3 tablespoons butter, 3 tablespoons flour, and 1 1/2 cups beef broth. Proceed with basic recipe.

southern grilled garlic porterhouse
Replace the beer-butter mixture with a marinade made by mixing together 1 cup Italian salad dressing, 1 cup barbecue sauce, 1/2 cup Worcestershire sauce, and 2 pressed large cloves garlic. Marinate steaks for 2 hours. Proceed with basic recipe.

marinated grilled porterhouse
Replace the beer-butter mixture with a marinade made by mixing together 1/4 cup olive oil; 2 tablespoons each of pressed fresh garlic, balsamic vinegar, and fresh lemon juice; and the finely chopped leaves of 1 sprig fresh rosemary. Marinate steaks for 2 hours. Proceed with basic recipe.

porterhouse steaks with bourbon and shallot sauce
Replace the beer-butter mixture with a marinade made by mixing together 1/2 cup sweet mustard, 1/2 cup bourbon, 1/4 cup shallots, and salt to taste. Marinate steaks for 2 hours. Proceed with basic recipe.

the ultimate steakhouse burger

see base recipe page 158

hamburgers with "hot" barbecue sauce
Make a sauce for the burgers by simmering together for 10 minutes the following ingredients: 1 cup ketchup; 1/4 cup white vinegar; 3 tablespoons each of Worcestershire sauce and light brown sugar; and 2 tablespoons each of water and prepared horseradish. Mix well and serve warm.

healthy grilled burgers
Omit the burger ingredients and bacon slices. Replace with a mixture of 1/2 pound each of ground turkey thigh meat, dried breadcrumbs, soft tofu, and grated carrots; 1 cup minced watercress; 1 minced small onion; and salt and pepper to taste. Garnish as in the base recipe.

new mexico green chili burgers
Omit garnishes. Instead, garnish each burger with sliced Monterey Jack cheese, canned green chilies, sliced red onion, sliced tomato, shredded romaine leaves, and fresh salsa.

french bistro burger
Omit the bacon slices and other garnishes. Top the burger with walnuts, Gruyère cheese, and garlic mustard mayonnaise. Serve on a French roll.

the ultimate lamb burger
Omit the bacon. Replace the ground beef and garlic with 1 1/2 pounds lean ground lamb and 1 1/2 teaspoons dried mint. Garnish as in the base recipe.

beer-marinated peppered t-bones

see base recipe page 161

grilled t-bones with cowboy grilled onions

Omit the marinade. Serve the grilled steaks topped with 4 sliced and grilled red onions, 1 cup barbecue sauce, and 4 grilled and sliced tomatoes.

company-coming t-bones

Replace the marinade with one made by combining 1 cup each of red wine and Worcestershire sauce, 2 tablespoons light brown sugar, and 1 tablespoon liquid smoke.

t-bones and wild mushroom medley

Omit the beer marinade. Serve the grilled steaks with a mushroom medley made by cooking together in a skillet the following: 2 ounces each of butter, chanterelles, champignons, and morel mushrooms, or mushrooms of your choice; 1 tablespoon chopped fresh parsley leaves; 1/2 cup brandy; and 1 tablespoon Worcestershire sauce. Cook until tender. Add 4 ounces heavy cream and reduce over a high heat to make a thick sauce. Serve with Dijon mustard.

t-bone à la blue

Omit the beer marinade. Serve grilled steaks with a flavored butter topping made by blending together 1/2 pound crumbled blue cheese, 1/2 pound softened unsalted butter, 1/2 cup breadcrumbs, 2 pressed large garlic cloves, and 1 teaspoon cracked black pepper.

t-bones el paso

Replace the marinade with one made by combining 1 envelope taco seasoning, 1/4 cup olive oil, and 1 tablespoon pressed garlic.

variations

grilled marinated sirloin steak

see base recipe page 162

steak and baby portobellos
Replace the marinade with one made by combining 1 cup Italian salad dressing, 1/2 cup dry
red wine, 1/2 cup grated onion, 3 pressed large cloves garlic, and 2 tablespoons chopped
fresh oregano. Marinate the steak in this mixture, along with 3 quartered sweet red peppers
and 8 ounces baby portobello mushrooms. Grill steak, peppers, and portobellos together.

peppered steak with tarragon
Replace the marinade with a paste made by mixing 3 tablespoons olive oil; 1 tablespoon
green peppercorns, drained and smashed; 3 large cloves garlic, pressed; and 2 tablespoons
chopped fresh tarragon. Proceed as in basic recipe.

grilled steaks with martini twist
Replace marinade with a mixture of 1/4 cup finely chopped green onions, 1/4 cup
gin, 1 tablespoon olive oil, 1 teaspoon grated lemon zest, 1 teaspoon freshly ground
tricolored peppercorns, and 2 tablespoons sliced pimento-stuffed green olives. Proceed as
in basic recipe.

korean bulgogi
Replace marinade with a mixture of 1 cup sesame oil, 2 cups soy sauce, 4 pressed large
cloves garlic, 1 tablespoon grated fresh gingerroot, and crushed red pepper flakes to taste.
Proceed as in basic recipe.

variations

balsamic hanger steaks

see base recipe page 163

hanger steaks with shallots
Omit the marinade and baste. Grill steaks as in the basic recipe. Make a sauce for the sliced grilled steak by sautéing 2 tablespoons unsalted butter, 1 cup thinly sliced shallots, 2 tablespoons red wine vinegar, 1 cup dry red wine, and 2 tablespoons chopped Italian parsley leaves. Cook until reduced to a thick sauce.

grilled hanger steaks
Omit the marinade and baste. Simply grill the steaks, seasoning them afterward with salt and pepper.

hanger steaks with mustard jus
Omit the marinade and baste. Instead make a marinade from 1/2 cup grapefruit juice, 1/4 cup red wine vinegar, and 2 grated shallots. Serve steak with a sauce made by simmering together until reduced by half: 1 tablespoon canola oil, 4 slivered shallots, 1/2 cup beef consommé, 1/2 cup red wine, 2 tablespoons sweet rice wine, 1 tablespoon Dijon mustard, and sugar to taste.

herbed hanger steaks
Omit the marinade and baste. Instead drizzle 3 tablespoons olive oil over the cooked steaks and sprinkle them with 1 tablespoon fresh thyme leaves and 4 thinly sliced large shallots.

tenderloin with herbed cheese

see base recipe page 164

romanian beef tenderloin
Omit the cheese mixture. Instead marinate the tenderloin and 4 large portobello mushrooms in a mixture of 1 cup canola oil, 1/2 cup olive oil, and 8 pressed large cloves garlic.

beef tenderloin with mustard tarragon cream sauce
Omit the cheese mixture, garlic rub, and parsley garnish. Instead make a sauce for the grilled tenderloin by blending well 1/4 cup dry white wine, 1/4 cup sour cream, 1 tablespoon each of Dijon mustard and sugar, and 1 1/2 teaspoons chopped fresh tarragon.

grilled southwestern bacon-wrapped beef tenderloin
Omit the cheese mixture, garlic rub, and parsley garnish. Instead wrap each tenderloin in a thick slice bacon. Make a rub by combining 1 tablespoon ground cumin, 1 tablespoon chili powder, 1 1/2 teaspoons paprika, 1/2 teaspoon cayenne, 1/4 teaspoon dried thyme, 1/4 teaspoon ground cinnamon, and 2 tablespoons canola oil. Rub mixture all over the meat and let stand for 30 minutes, before grilling as in the basic recipe. Garnish grilled tenderloins with chopped fresh cilantro.

grilled beef tenderloin
Omit the cheese mixture, garlic rub, and parsley garnish. Instead make a rub by combining 2 teaspoons dried rosemary, 1 teaspoon dried thyme, 1 teaspoon dried tarragon, and 2 pressed large cloves garlic. Rub mixture all over the meat and let stand for 30 minutes, before grilling as in the basic recipe.

variations

grilled flank steak with aïoli

see base recipe page 167

grilled flank steak with almond-cilantro pesto
Instead of the aïoli, mix the following to make a rub: 1 teaspoon each of sea salt, black pepper, ground cumin, ground coriander, and garlic powder; and 1/4 teaspoon chili powder. Rub into the meat and let stand for 30 minutes. Grill as in the basic recipe. Serve with a pesto made by mixing 2 tablespoons toasted slivered almonds; 1/2 cup each of fresh cilantro and parsley leaves; 1 tablespoon each of chopped and seeded jalapeño and fresh lime juice; 2 pressed cloves garlic; 1/4 teaspoon each of salt and black pepper; and 1/4 cup sour cream.

santa fe flank steak
Instead of the aïoli, blend the following to make a marinade: 1/4 cup canola oil, 2 tablespoons each of chopped fresh cilantro and parsley, 4 pressed large cloves garlic, 2 teaspoons each of sea salt and ground cumin, and 1 teaspoon each of ground coriander, cayenne, and black pepper. Marinate steak for 2 hours.

caribbean jerk beef steak
Instead of the aïoli, blend the following to make a marinade: 1 cup Italian salad dressing; 2 tablespoons Worcestershire sauce; 1 tablespoon light brown sugar; 1 large jalapeño, seeded and chopped; and 1 teaspoon each of ground allspice and ginger. Marinate steak for 2 hours.

grilled flank steak with nectarines
Omit the aïoli. Marinate the steak for 2 hours in 1/4 cup each of red wine, soy sauce, chicken broth, and clover honey, and 1 teaspoon ground ginger. Serve with 4 halved, grilled nectarines.

béarnaise butter

see base recipe page 168

blue cheese, rosemary, and balsamic vinegar butter
Instead of making the béarnaise butter, stir the following into the same quantity of butter: 2 tablespoons each of minced fresh rosemary leaves, and balsamic vinegar, 1 teaspoon Worcestershire sauce, 1 pressed large clove garlic, 1/2 cup crumbled blue cheese, 1/2 teaspoon sea salt, and 1/4 teaspoon freshly ground black pepper.

maître d'hôtel butter (the king of steak butters)
Instead of making the béarnaise butter, stir the following into the same quantity of butter: 1/4 cup chopped fresh parsley, 4 teaspoons fresh lemon juice, 1/2 teaspoon sea salt, and 1/4 teaspoon freshly ground black pepper.

chipotle chili steak butter
Instead of making the béarnaise butter, stir the following into the same quantity of butter: 2 tablespoons minced shallots; 1 tablespoon each of chopped fresh cilantro and minced chipotle peppers in adobo sauce, seeded; 1 teaspoon fresh lime juice; 1 teaspoon grated lime zest, 1/2 teaspoon sea salt; and 1/4 teaspoon freshly ground black pepper.

pesto-walnut butter
Instead of making the béarnaise butter, stir the following into the same quantity of butter: 3 tablespoons each of prepared basil pesto and minced toasted walnuts, 1/2 teaspoon sea salt, and 1/4 teaspoon freshly ground black pepper.

variations

strip steak simple

see base recipe page 169

the perfect strip steak
Add a marinade. Combine 2 pressed cloves garlic; 2 tablespoons each of Worcestershire sauce, soy sauce, balsamic vinegar, and olive oil; and 1 tablespoon Dijon mustard. Marinate steaks for 2 hours, and proceed with the base recipe.

coffee bean and gourmet peppercorn crusted steak
Add a crust: crush 1/4 cup toasted gourmet peppercorns and 1/4 cup dark-roasted coffee beans; press into the steaks before grilling. Proceed with the base recipe.

mango strip steak
Add a marinade. Heat the following ingredients in a skillet for 10 minutes: 1/2 cup each of diced mango, apple, and honeydew melon; 2 tablespoons each Worcestershire sauce and garlic salt; and 1 teaspoon black pepper. Marinate steaks for 2 hours, and proceed with the base recipe.

steak au poivre rouge
Add a crust: crush 4 tablespoons black peppercorns, 1 tablespoon white peppercorns, and 1 teaspoon kosher salt; press into the steaks. Proceed with the base recipe. Combine 8 tablespoons softened unsalted butter, 1/2 cup very hearty red wine, and 1 tablespoon chopped fresh chives. Top the steaks with this butter when serving.

barbecued baby beef ribs

see base recipe page 171

big bill's beef ribs
Replace the rub with one made by mixing 1/4 cup kosher salt; 2 tablespoons each of paprika and coarse ground black pepper; 1 1/2 teaspoons each of garlic powder, onion powder, and cayenne pepper; and 1/2 teaspoon each of ground coriander and turmeric.

beef ribs with chinese spices
Replace the mop with one made by mixing 1/2 cup hoisin sauce, 1/4 cup sweet rice wine vinegar, 2 tablespoons clover honey, 2 pressed cloves garlic, and 1 tablespoon grated fresh ginger. Replace the rub with one made by mixing 2 tablespoons kosher salt, 1 tablespoon each of coarse ground black pepper and Chinese five-spice powder, 2 teaspoons garlic powder, and 1 teaspoon ground ginger.

tender smoked beef ribs
Replace the rub with one made by combining 1/4 cup sugar; 2 tablespoons each of onion powder, garlic powder, kosher salt, and Old Bay Seasoning; 1 tablespoon each of black pepper and paprika; 2 teaspoons each of seasoned salt and dried oregano; and 1/2 teaspoon each of dried sage, grated nutmeg, and cayenne.

jack's barbecued sweet beef ribs
Replace the mop with a sauce made by simmering together for 20 minutes 1 cup ketchup; 1/4 cup each of cider vinegar and water; 2 tablespoons each of Worcestershire sauce and brown sugar; 1 tablespoon onion powder; and 1 teaspoon each of dry mustard and paprika.

variations

grilled chilean skirt steak

see base recipe page 175

spicy grilled skirt steak
Instead of cumin and cilantro, flavor the marinade with 1 tablespoon ground coriander. Replace the relish with one made by combining 1 large red onion, sliced thin; 1 sweet red pepper, seeded and sliced thin; and 3 tablespoons hot taco sauce or to taste.

grilled garlic skirt steak
Replace the marinade with one made by combining 6 pressed large cloves garlic, 1 teaspoon dry mustard, 1 teaspoon ground cumin, 1/2 teaspoon powdered bay leaf, 1/4 cup Worcestershire sauce, 1/4 cup cider vinegar, 1 tablespoon canola oil, 1 tablespoon Louisiana hot sauce, and 1 cup boiling beef broth. Omit the relish.

new mexico grilled skirt steak
Replace the marinade with one made by combining 3 tablespoons New Mexican chili powder; 1 tablespoon each of ground cumin, garlic powder, and sugar; 2 teaspoons black pepper; 1 teaspoon ground allspice; 1/4 cup Worcestershire sauce; and 2 tablespoons canola oil. Retain the relish from the base recipe.

amarillo texas marinated skirt steak
Replace the marinade with one made by combining 1/4 cup fresh lemon juice, 1/4 cup olive oil, 1 tablespoon ground cumin, 2 teaspoons chili powder, and 1 teaspoon chipotle powder. Retain the relish from the base recipe.

variations

grilled veal chops with rosemary

see base recipe page 177

the baron's grilled veal chops
Replace the rosemary marinade with one made by mixing 1/4 cup olive oil with
2 tablespoons each of balsamic vinegar, kosher salt, coarse ground black pepper, minced
dried garlic, and crushed rosemary. Blend well.

grilled basil veal chops
Replace the rosemary marinade with one made by mixing 3 tablespoons balsamic
vinegar, 1/4 cup fresh lemon juice, 1/4 cup olive oil, 1/3 cup chopped fresh basil leaves,
1 tablespoon each of lemon zest and chopped shallots, 4 pressed cloves garlic, and salt
and pepper to taste.

grilled lemon-herb veal chops
Replace the rosemary marinade with one made by mixing 3 tablespoons each of olive oil
and fresh lemon juice, 3 pressed cloves garlic, 1 tablespoon minced fresh oregano leaves,
and 1 teaspoon freshly ground black pepper.

grilled veal chops with roasted garlic paste
Omit the rosemary marinade. Grill the chops as in the base recipe. Make a spice paste
by mixing 1/4 cup roasted garlic, 3 tablespoons softened butter, 2 tablespoons olive oil,
2 tablespoons Dijon mustard, and 1 teaspoon chipotle powder. Rub this paste onto the
grilled chops before serving.

variations

barbecued short ribs

see base recipe page 178

red wine short ribs

Replace the rub with a marinade made by mixing 1/2 cup dry red wine, 1/4 cup soy sauce, 2 tablespoons canola oil, 3 pressed cloves garlic, 1/2 teaspoon dried thyme, and 1/2 teaspoon freshly ground black pepper. Marinate ribs for 2 hours, and proceed with the base recipe.

grilled korean short ribs

Replace the rub with a marinade made by mixing 1/2 cup soy sauce, 1/2 cup dry sherry, 1/4 cup pineapple juice, 2 tablespoons each of sesame oil and sugar, and 1 tablespoon grated fresh gingerroot. Marinate ribs for 2 hours, and proceed with the base recipe.

grilled texas beef short ribs

Replace the rub with a marinade made by mixing 1/2 cup flat bock beer; 1/4 cup each of olive oil, brown sugar, and balsamic vinegar; 2 tablespoons each of chili powder, seeded and chopped jalapeño, molasses, and grated onion; 6 pressed cloves garlic, 1 tablespoon coarse ground black pepper; and 2 teaspoons sea salt. Marinate ribs for 2 hours, and proceed with the base recipe.

spicy kansas city grilled beef short ribs

Replace the rub with a Kansas City rub made by mixing 1/4 cup light brown sugar; 2 tablespoons each of garlic salt and seasoned salt; 1 tablespoon chili powder; 1 teaspoon each of ground allspice, black pepper, ground cumin, and ground ginger; 1/2 teaspoon chipotle powder; and 1/2 teaspoon ground cinnamon.

variations

grilled tri-tip roast

see base recipe page 179

tasty tequila tri-tip
Replace the rub with a marinade made by mixing 1/4 cup tequila; 2 tablespoons each
of sesame oil, Dijon mustard, and balsamic vinegar; 2 pressed large cloves garlic; and
2 teaspoons each of sea salt and freshly ground black pepper. Marinate for 2 hours, and
proceed with the base recipe.

spicy grilled beef tri-tip
Substitute the following for the rub ingredients: 2 tablespoons onion powder, 2 tablespoons
packed light brown sugar, 1 tablespoon paprika, 1 tablespoon chili powder, 1 teaspoon
cayenne, sea salt to taste, and 1/2 teaspoon each of ground cumin and cinnamon.

marinated tri-tip
Replace the rub with a marinade made by mixing 1/2 cup burgundy wine, 1/2 cup teriyaki
sauce, 1/4 cup canola oil, 1/4 cup soy sauce, 1/3 cup red wine vinegar, 1 tablespoon paprika,
1 tablespoon crushed dried parsley flakes, and 3 pressed large cloves garlic. Marinate for
2 hours, and proceed with the base recipe.

santa maria-style grilled tri-tip
Replace the rub with one made by mixing 6 tablespoons kosher salt, 4 tablespoons garlic
powder, 2 tablespoons paprika, 1 tablespoon each of coarse ground black pepper and white
pepper, 2 teaspoons cayenne pepper, and 1 teaspoon onion powder. While grilling, baste with
a mixture of 1/2 cup red wine vinegar and 1/2 cup garlic-infused vegetable oil.

vegetarian bites

Fresh vegetables with a seared crusty edge are one

of the most appetizing elements of any barbecue.

Try your hand at some of our simple veggie grills, or

make them the centerpiece of your meal by putting

together a colorful assorted platter.

grilled lollipop onions

see variations page 219

Grilled onions lose their acrid flavor, becoming soft and smoky with a sweet edge.

2 sweet onions, e.g. Walla-Walla, Vidalia, Texas
    sweet, or Maui (about 1 1/2 lbs. total),
    peeled, sliced 1/2-in. thick
8 to 12 grilling skewers

Sea salt and freshly ground black pepper to
    taste
2 tbsp. canola oil

Preheat a grill to medium. Insert 2 skewers parallel, 1 inch apart, through the onion slices. Season both sides of the onions with salt and pepper; brush with canola oil. Be careful: too much oil will cause flare-ups on the grill.

Grill the onions, covered, for about 5 minutes. Turn over; brush with canola oil; and grill for 5 to 7 more minutes or until tender.

Serves 8–12

roasted garlic grilled tomatoes

see variations page 220

The appetizing scents of an Italian kitchen will draw your guests to the barbecue when you prepare these simple yet sophisticated tomatoes..

6 ripe tomatoes
Coarse salt and black pepper
3 tbsp. extra-virgin olive oil
2 tbsp. butter, melted

8 cloves roasted garlic
1 to 2 oz. Parmesan cheese
1 tsp. dried thyme leaves

Cut the tomatoes in half crosswise. Season with salt and pepper, and set aside. Heat the oil and butter in a small skillet. Add the roasted garlic and cook until well blended and incorporated, 1 to 2 minutes. Pour the garlic mixture into a heatproof bowl.

Preheat a grill to high. If using a gas grill, place wood chips, if desired, in the smoker box or a smoker pouch and preheat until you see smoke. If using a charcoal grill, toss the wood chips, if desired, on the coals. Place the tomatoes cut-side down on the hot grate and grill until nicely browned, 3 to 5 minutes, rotating them 45 degrees after 2 minutes to create an attractive crosshatch of grill marks. Turn the tomatoes with tongs, spoon the fried garlic over the tomatoes, and continue grilling until the bottoms are nicely browned, 3 to 5 minutes.

Transfer the tomatoes to a platter. Grate the Parmesan over the tomatoes and sprinkle them with the thyme. Serve at once.

Serves 3

spicy grilled eggplant

see variations page 221

Fresh herbs and a squeeze of lemon make a vibrant partnership with the smoky taste of grilled eggplant.

1 globe eggplant or 2-3 long Asian eggplants, cut into 1/2-in.-thick slices
1-2 tsp. salt, to remove water from eggplant
2 tbsp. olive oil
2 tsp. red wine vinegar
2 tsp. fresh lemon juice
1 tsp. pressed garlic

1 tsp. crushed red pepper flakes
1 tsp. Spike seasoning
2 tbsp. olive oil, to brush eggplant for grilling
1 tbsp. chopped fresh parsley
1 tbsp. chopped fresh mint

Put the eggplant slices in a colander in a single layer and sprinkle with salt. Let drain for 20 minutes, then turn, sprinkle the other side with salt, and let drain 20 minutes more. (If you're using Asian eggplant, there's no need to salt.) While the eggplant drains, whisk together the olive oil, wine vinegar, lemon juice, garlic, red pepper, and Spike. Set the spicy sauce aside.

Preheat a grill to medium. Press each eggplant slice between 2 pieces of paper toweling to dry them. Brush both sides with the 2 tablespoons olive oil. Place the eggplant on the grill and cook 4 to 5 minutes per side, rotating after a few minutes on each side if you want to get grill marks. Watch them carefully because they go from gently browned to charred quickly. When the eggplant is done, remove from the grill and place in a large plastic bowl. Stir in the spicy sauce to coat. Let sit. Sprinkle the parsley and mint over the eggplant and serve warm or at room temperature.

Serves 4

grilled sweet potatoes

see variations page 222

Parboiling before grilling cuts down the actual grilling time, making this a quick and simple vegetable dish.

4 to 6 medium sweet potatoes (or yams),
    scrubbed
1/4 cup canola oil
Sea salt and freshly ground pepper to taste

Parboil the potatoes for 10 minutes, then allow them to cool. Cut each one into 6 or 8 wedges or slices. Brush the potatoes all over with oil. Grill over medium heat for 5 to 7 minutes per side until crisp and lightly browned. Season as desired.

Serves 4–6

grilled herbed potatoes

see variations page 223

Turn the potatoes through 90 degrees halfway through cooking to obtain attractive chargrilled scorch marks on all the slices.

4 medium potatoes, brushed and washed
2 tbsp. olive oil
1 cup thinly sliced green onions
4 tbsp. olive oil
3 tbsp. grated Parmesan cheese

3 tbsp. chopped fresh parsley
2 tbsp. chopped fresh oregano
3 cloves garlic, pressed
Salt and pepper to taste

Cook the potatoes in a large pot of boiling salt water until tender. Drain and cool. Cut the potatoes into wedges or slices and place in a large bowl. Add 2 tablespoons of olive oil and toss to mix.

Grill the potatoes on a grill preheated to medium for 5 minutes, turning occasionally. Transfer to a bowl. Add the remaining ingredients and toss to mix. Season with salt and pepper to taste.

Serves 4

asparagus with black pepper

see variations page 224

A vegetable as elegant as asparagus suits simple preparations like this one.

1 lb. asparagus
Sea salt and freshly ground black pepper
**   to taste**

Snap or cut off any dry ends from the asparagus spears; soak them in cold water for 30 minutes. Cook on a grill preheated to medium until the ends begin to soften. Turn perpendicularly across the grill to obtain grill marks, being careful not to let the spears fall through.

Be careful not to overcook the spears or to let the outside burn. Season with sea salt and freshly ground black pepper to taste.

Serves 4

grilled patty pan squash

see variations page 225

These tiny squash are available in a range of colors. Use a mixture if possible to make this dish even more bright and attractive.

1/4 cup olive oil
2 tsp. grated onion
1 tsp. dried sweet marjoram
1 large clove garlic, pressed
12 small patty pan squash

Combine the olive oil and all of the flavorings, blend well, and set aside.

Cut the squash lengthwise and remove the seeds. Wash thoroughly in cold water and pat dry. Preheat a grill to medium. Brush the squash on one side with olive oil mixture and place face down on the grill.

Cover and cook for 6 to 10 minutes. Brush the top of the squash with the olive oil mixture, turn over, and cover again. Repeat this process until the squash is golden brown on both sides.

Serve hot, sprinkled with the cheese of your choice if you like.

Serves 6

grilled vegetable platter with balsamic maple dressing

see variations page 226

The bright colors of the vegetables piled high on this platter look really spectacular.

1 lb. thick asparagus spears
2 zucchini
1 bunch carrots (about 8 oz.), peeled
1 red bell pepper
1 yellow bell pepper
1 large red onion, peeled
2 tbsp. vegetable oil

1 tbsp. fresh thyme
Sea salt and freshly ground black pepper to
    taste
1/2 cup balsamic vinegar
1/4 cup maple syrup

Trim the woody ends of the asparagus spears. Cut the zucchini and carrots lengthwise into thirds. Seed and core the red and yellow peppers; cut each into eighths. Set the onion on its root end and cut it into 8 wedges, leaving the end intact. Place the vegetables in a bowl. Toss the vegetables with the oil, thyme, salt, and pepper. Place the vegetables on a grill preheated to medium. Close the lid and cook for 3 minutes. Remove the asparagus and keep warm. Rotate the remaining vegetables 90 degrees to make crosshatched grill marks. Cover the grill again. Continue cooking, rotating every 3 minutes, until tender-crisp. Remove from the heat.

Meanwhile, in a small saucepan, bring vinegar and maple syrup to boil; boil until thickened, about 2 minutes. Brush one-quarter of the glaze over vegetables; turn over and brush again. Transfer to a serving platter and brush with remaining glaze.

Serves 6

vegetable kabobs

see variations page 227

Kabobs are too often thought of as being for carnivores only. Try these sweet skewered vegetables and you'll soon see how wrong that thinking is.

1 eggplant, cut into cubes
1 sweet red pepper, sliced in 1-in. strips
8 small onions, peeled
16 medium-sized button mushrooms
8 cherry tomatoes
1 medium cucumber, cut into 8 slices
1 stalk celery cut into 1-in. pieces
Water-soaked skewers

1/2 cup fresh lemon juice
Grated zest of 2 lemons
1 tbsp. olive oil
2 pressed large cloves garlic
1 tbsp. chopped fresh thyme
1 cup chopped fresh herbs of your choice
Salt and freshly ground black pepper to taste

Thread the vegetables on skewers, alternating the colors to make them look more attractive, and place on a large dish. Sprinkle with the lemon juice and zest, oil, garlic, and thyme. Marinate for 1 hour, turning occasionally. Preheat the grill to medium.

Before grilling, roll the skewers in your favorite combination of fresh herbs. Place the skewers directly on the grill, about 3 to 4 inches from the heat source. Cover and grill for 15 to 20 minutes or until tender and brown, turning frequently.

Serves 4–6

creole-style stuffed mushrooms

see variations page 228

The type of mushrooms you choose will determine how much filling you will need, so adjust the recipes as needed.

1 lb. button mushrooms
1 tsp. olive oil
1/4 cup minced onion
1/4 cup minced red bell pepper
10-oz. package frozen spinach, thawed and
    drained

2 1/2 slices whole wheat bread, torn into
    breadcrumbs
1 tsp. Creole or Cajun seasoning
1/4 tsp. ground turmeric
1/4 cup Monterey Jack cheese, shredded

Preheat your smoker to 250°F (120°C). Lightly coat a sheet pan or mini-muffin pans with cooking spray. Remove the mushroom stems from caps. Finely chop the stems. Reserve the caps and set aside.

Heat the olive oil in a large skillet over high heat. Sauté the chopped mushroom stems, onion, pepper, and spinach until tender, about 5 minutes. Remove the skillet from the heat and stir in the breadcrumbs and seasonings until well combined.

Stuff each mushroom cap with 2 tablespoons of the filling mixture. Place the mushrooms, stuffed sides up, on the sheet pan. Place in the smoker and cook for about 45 minutes to 1 hour. A few minutes before the end of cooking, remove from the grill and sprinkle the cheese on the top. Place back in the smoker to finish cooking. Serve warm.

Serves 2–3

grape-nuts burgers

see variations page 229

You could use any crunchy, not-too-sweet breakfast cereal if Grape-Nuts are unavailable.

2 eggs, well beaten
1/2 cup V-8 juice
1 envelope dry onion soup mix
1/3 cup ketchup
2 cups Grape-Nuts cereal

Sea salt and freshly ground black pepper
Cooking spray
Wholegrain buns, toasted
Garnish: lettuce, sliced onions, and sliced tomatoes

In a large bowl, whisk together the eggs, V-8 juice, onion soup mix, and ketchup. Work in the cereal. The mixture will resemble meatloaf. Cover and refrigerate for 4 or 5 hours or overnight. Form into 8 patties.

Prepare a medium-hot grill. Spray the burgers with cooking spray and grill over medium heat, covered, for about 4 to 5 minutes on each side. Spray the top of the burgers before turning. Let brown on each side. Using a grill basket will make turning these much easier. Serve on buns and garnish with lettuce, sliced onions, and sliced tomatoes.

Makes 8

variations

grilled lollipop onions

see base recipe page 199

grilled red onions
Replace the sweet onions with halved medium red onions. Omit canola oil, salt, and pepper. Instead, marinate onions for 2 hours in a mixture made from 2 tablespoons each of Worcestershire sauce, balsamic vinegar, soy sauce, and olive oil; with sea salt and freshly ground black pepper to taste. Drain before grilling.

zesty grilled baby onions
Replace the sweet onions with 24 baby onions, parboiled for 5 minutes. Place them on 4 bamboo skewers. Omit canola oil, salt, and pepper. Instead, brush them with a mixture made from 1/4 cup Italian dressing, 1/4 cup sweet onion salad dressing, 8 tablespoons melted unsalted butter, and kosher salt and coarse ground black pepper to taste. Baste.

mexican grilled onions
Prepare the base recipe, seasoning the onions before grilling with taco seasoning to taste.

beer and cayenne grilled onions
Omit canola oil, salt, and pepper. Marinate the sliced onions for 2 hours in a mixture of a 12-ounce can beer; 1/2 cup melted unsalted butter; 2 tablespoons olive oil; and sea salt, freshly ground black pepper, and cayenne to taste. Drain, reserving the marinade. Skewer and grill as in the base recipe, using the marinade to baste regularly.

variations

roasted garlic grilled tomatoes

see base recipe page 200

grilled green tomatoes
Omit the roasted garlic, oil, and butter. Replace the red tomatoes with 4 large green tomatoes, sliced 1/2-inch thick. Make a topping or dip by combining 1/4 cup each of sour cream, mayonnaise, and Louisiana hot sauce.

grilled tomato melts
Omit the roasted garlic, oil, butter, Parmesan, and thyme. Five minutes before the end of grilling, top the tomatoes with 1 1/2 cups shredded Monterey Jack cheese, 1/2 cup chopped sweet red pepper, and 1/4 cup toasted sliced almonds.

herb-grilled tomatoes
Omit the roasted garlic, oil, butter, Parmesan and thyme. Replace the fried garlic topping with a mixture of 1/2 cup sour cream or plain yogurt and 3 tablespoons each of chopped fresh basil, fine dry breadcrumbs, and finely grated Parmesan cheese. Garnish with 4 to 5 sprigs fresh basil.

spicy grilled tomatoes
Omit everything except the tomatoes. Replace the fried garlic topping with a mixture of 1 serrano chili, seeded and minced; 1 cup plain yogurt; and 1 teaspoon each of onion powder, sugar, and curry powder. Use as a topping for the grilled tomatoes.

variations

spicy grilled eggplant

see base recipe page 203

honey-garlic grilled eggplant
Omit the olive oil for brushing onto the eggplant. Replace the herbs and the spicy sauce with
a marinade made by mixing 2 tablespoons clover honey, 2 tablespoons olive oil, 2 pressed
large cloves garlic, 1 tablespoon smoked paprika, 2 teaspoons balsamic vinegar, and salt and
pepper to taste. Marinate for 2 hours. Drain and cook, basting with the reserved marinade.

herb and garlic grilled eggplant
Omit the olive oil for brushing onto the eggplant. Replace the herbs and the spicy sauce with
a marinade made by mixing 2/3 cup extra-virgin olive oil, 4 pressed large cloves garlic,
1/2 tightly packed cup each of chopped fresh basil and Italian parsley leaves, salt to taste,
and 1/8 teaspoon freshly ground black pepper. Marinate for 2 hours. Drain and cook, basting
with the reserved marinade.

grilled eggplant
Omit the olive oil for brushing onto the eggplant. Replace the herbs and the spicy sauce with
a marinade made by mixing 3 tablespoons olive oil; 2 tablespoons balsamic vinegar; 2 cloves
garlic, very finely minced; 1 pinch each of dried thyme, basil, dill, and oregano; and salt and
pepper to taste. Marinate for 2 hours. Drain and cook, basting with the reserved marinade.

garlic-butter grilled eggplant
Omit the olive oil for brushing onto the eggplant. Replace the herbs and spicy sauce with a
baste: combine 8 tablespoons butter at room temperature and 4 pressed cloves garlic.

variations

grilled sweet potatoes

see base recipe page 204

grilled sweet potato sticks
Place the potato or yam pieces on 4 water-soaked bamboo skewers. Instead of the oil, brush the potatoes with 2/3 cup melted butter, 2 tablespoons soy sauce, and 1 tablespoon toasted sesame seeds. Grill like kabobs, turning regularly.

grilled candied sweet potatoes
Omit the canola oil. Stir together 1/4 cup light brown sugar and 2 tablespoons lemon juice. Grill the potatoes or yams as in the base recipe, brushing regularly with the sugar and lemon mixture so that they form a caramelized crust.

jamaican grilled sweet potatoes
Omit the canola oil. Stir together 1/4 cup packed light brown sugar, 2 tablespoons softened butter, 1 teaspoon ground ginger, 1/2 teaspoon ground allspice, 1 tablespoon dark rum, and 1 tablespoon chopped fresh cilantro. Grill the potatoes or yams as in the base recipe, brushing regularly with this mixture while cooking.

cinnamon-grilled sweet potatoes
Omit the canola oil. Stir together 2/3 cup melted butter, 2 tablespoons sugar, and 1 teaspoon cinnamon sugar. Grill the potatoes or yams as in the base recipe, brushing regularly with this mixture while cooking.

grilled herbed potatoes

see base recipe page 207

grilled potatoes tuscan-style
Replace the onions, cheese, parsley, and oregano with 5 chopped fresh sage leaves and 2 teaspoons chopped fresh rosemary. Proceed with the base recipe.

grilled potatoes with roasted garlic
Replace the 4 tablespoons olive oil, onions, cheese, parsley, oregano, and garlic with 2 heads smoked or roasted garlic, blended to a paste with 1/4 cup extra-virgin olive oil. Garnish cooked potatoes with 2 tablespoons chopped fresh parsley. Proceed with the base recipe.

honey-grilled potatoes
Replace the onions, cheese, parsley, oregano, and garlic with 2 tablespoons diced onions, 2 tablespoons clover honey, and 1 teaspoon dry mustard. Proceed with the base recipe.

simple grilled potatoes
Replace the onions, cheese, garlic, oregano, and parsley with 2 teaspoons seasoned salt. Replace the 4 tablespoons olive oil with 1/4 cup melted butter. Proceed with the base recipe.

scandinavian herbed potatoes
Omit the onions, cheese, oil, herbs, and garlic. Replace them with 3 tablespoons chopped fresh dill and 8 crushed juniper berries. Proceed with the base recipe.

variations

asparagus with black pepper

see base recipe page 208

asparagus with honey-garlic sauce
Prepare the base recipe. Serve the grilled asparagus with a sauce made by stirring together 1/4 cup Dijon mustard, 1/4 cup dark ale or dark beer, 3 tablespoons clover honey, 1 teaspoon pressed garlic, and 1/4 teaspoon dried thyme.

grilled sesame asparagus
Prepare the base recipe. Serve the grilled asparagus with a sauce made by stirring together 2 tablespoons soy sauce, 2 tablespoons sweet rice wine vinegar, 1 tablespoon toasted sesame oil, 1 tablespoon sesame seeds, and 1 finely chopped jalapeño.

grilled asparagus with red onion and orange
Prepare the base recipe, basting the asparagus while grilling with a mixture of 1/4 cup diced celery, 1/4 cup diced red onion, 1 tablespoon grated carrot, 1 tablespoon peeled and grated gingerroot, 1 teaspoon grated orange zest, 1/3 cup unsweetened apple juice, 2 tablespoons rice vinegar, and 1 tablespoon clover honey. Drizzle any excess basting mixture over the finished asparagus.

grilled asparagus with red pepper sauce
Prepare the base recipe. Serve the grilled asparagus with a sauce made by stirring together 2 roasted sweet red peppers, chopped fine; 2 cloves garlic, pressed; 3 tablespoons red wine vinegar; 2 tablespoons olive oil; and 1/4 cup torn fresh basil leaves.

variations

grilled patty pan squash

see base recipe page 211

grilled squash
Omit the marjoram, garlic, and onion. Grill the squash as in the base recipe, basting regularly with 2 tablespoons melted butter in place of the oil.

oregano grilled squash
Omit the marjoram, garlic, and onion. Grill the squash as in the base recipe. Garnish the cooked squash with 1 tablespoon chopped fresh oregano.

onion and rosemary grilled squash
Replace the marjoram and onion with 2 red onions, cut into 3/4-inch slices; 1/2 teaspoon crushed red pepper flakes; and 1/2 teaspoon dried rosemary.

grilled squash parmesan
Replace the marjoram, garlic, and onion with 2 diced tomatoes and 1/2 teaspoon dried oregano. Before the last minute on the grill, sprinkle the squash with 1 cup grated Parmesan.

summertime grilled squash
Prepare the base recipe, pouring over the grilled squash a topping made by stirring 3 tablepoons chopped fresh mint into 1/2 cup plain yogurt.

grilled vegetable platter with balsamic maple dressing

see base recipe page 212

tuscan grilled summer vegetables
Add to the platter 3 sliced ripe tomatoes and 1 cup chopped fresh basil. Replace the dressing with a marinade made by mixing together 1/4 cup each of red wine, olive oil, chopped fresh sage, and chopped fresh rosemary; 1 tablespoon crushed black peppercorns; 1 tablespoon grated orange zest; and 2 pressed cloves garlic. Marinate the vegetables for 30 minutes. Drain, then grill as in the base recipe.

grilled vegetables with basil aïoli
Prepare the platter as in the base recipe. Replace the dressing with a basil aïoli made by whisking together 1/4 cup torn basil leaves, 2 pressed large cloves garlic, 1 egg yolk, 2 teaspoons fresh lemon juice, and 1/2 cup olive oil. The oil must be added gradually in a thin stream, not all at once. Put aïoli in a bowl to serve with the vegetables.

grilled vegetable platter with fresh basil vinaigrette
Prepare the platter as in the base recipe. Replace the dressing with a vinaigrette made by whisking together 1 cup extra-virgin olive oil, 1/4 cup fresh lemon juice, 1/4 cup finely chopped fresh basil, 2 pressed cloves garlic, and 1 tablespoon Dijon mustard.

mediterranean grilled vegetables
Marinate the vegetables for 30 minutes in a mixture of 1 cup olive oil and 1/3 cup Italian seasoning, before proceeding with the base recipe.

vegetable kabobs

see base recipe page 215

fruit and vegetable kabobs
Replace the lemon juice, zest, olive oil, garlic, and herbs with 3 tablespoons olive oil,
2 tablespoons cider vinegar, and 2 tablespoons orange juice. Alternate the vegetables on the
kabobs with 6 ounces dried apricots and 2 thickly sliced bananas.

vegetable kabobs with cherry tomatoes
Double the quantity of cherry tomatoes on the kabobs. Drizzle with olive oil after grilling.

teriyaki tofu and fruit kabobs
Omit the marinade. Replace the vegetables with 3/4 pound extra-firm tofu, drained and cut
into 32 cubes, and 1 cup canned pineapple chunks. Stir the following ingredients together to
use as a marinade: 1/2 cup orange juice, 2 tablespoons soy sauce, 2 tablespoons light brown
sugar, 2 pressed cloves garlic, and 1 tablespoon peeled and grated fresh gingerroot. Grill as in
the base recipe.

teriyaki kabobs
Add to the kabobs 2 ears corn, cut into 2-inch chunks. Grill as in the base recipe, basting
regularly with 1 cup teriyaki sauce.

vegetable kabobs with sour cream dressing
Prepare the base recipe. Alongside the kabobs, serve a bowl of dressing made by stirring
1 pressed clove garlic and 1 tablespoon chopped fresh chives into 1/2 cup sour cream.

variations

creole-style stuffed mushrooms

see base recipe page 216

grilled stuffed portobello mushrooms
Replace the red pepper, breadcrumbs, Cajun seasoning, turmeric, and cheese with 1 cup chopped fresh tomatoes; 1/4 cup each of sun-dried tomatoes and black olives; and 2 pressed cloves garlic. Retain the spinach and onion from the base recipe. Use to stuff portobello caps.

mushrooms napoleon
Replace the onions, spinach, red pepper, Cajun seasoning, turmeric, and cheese with 1 large tomato, seeded and diced; 3 tablespoons each of chopped flat-leaf parsley and extra-virgin olive oil; 1 tablespoon each of chopped fresh basil and red wine vinegar; 9 slices bread, torn into crumbs; and 1/2 cup shaved Asiago cheese. Garnish the cooked mushrooms with fresh basil sprigs.

cajun-style portobello mushrooms
Omit the stuffing and leave the mushroom stems intact. Omit the cheese. Grill the mushrooms as in the base recipe and season them afterward with 1 teaspoon Cajun seasoning. Drizzle over them a dressing made by combining 2 tablespoons Worcestershire sauce, 2 tablespoons balsamic vinegar, and 1 tablespoon olive oil.

paul's grilled mushrooms
Omit the stuffing, seasoning, and cheese. Leave the mushroom stems intact. Grill the mushrooms as in the base recipe and drizzle 1/2 cup Italian salad dressing over them after grilling.

variations

grape-nuts burgers

see base recipe page 218

veggie burgers
Replace the eggs, juice, soup mix, ketchup, and Grape-Nuts with a mixture of a 15-ounce can kidney beans, rinsed and drained; 1/2 cup each of rolled oats, chopped fresh mushrooms, chopped onion, and chopped red bell pepper; 1 grated carrot; and 2 pressed cloves garlic. Proceed with the base recipe.

zesty white bean burgers
Replace 1 of the eggs, the juice, soup mix, ketchup, and Grape-Nuts with a 15-ounce can great northern beans, mashed with a fork; a 5-ounce can chopped green chilies; 2 green onions, sliced thin; 1 cup dry breadcrumbs; and 1/4 cup yellow cornmeal. Proceed with the base recipe.

portobello mushroom sandwich
Replace the juice, soup mix, ketchup, and Grape-Nuts with 1 1/2 cups chopped portobello mushroom caps and 2 tablespoons olive oil. There is no need to refrigerate this mixture. Form into patties and grill as in the base recipe.

pepper sandwich
Omit the burger mixture. Make a different filling for the buns by grilling 2 red and 1 yellow bell peppers, seeded and sliced; and 1 large red onion, sliced 1/2-inch thick. Lay the grilled vegetables on the open buns and drizzle Italian salad dressing over them. Top with the remaining bun halves.

salads and sides

Cool crunchy salads and tasty side dishes complete
your barbecue feast. The dishes here are suited to
being served alongside any of the main dishes in
the earlier chapters. You could try Spanish coleslaw
for a light accompaniment to fish or steak or make
a vegetarian grill more substantial with a potato
salad or bean casserole.

potato salad with cucumber and dill

see variations page 248

The tangy combination of cucumber and dill adds a Scandinavian note to this otherwise classic potato salad.

3 lbs. new red potatoes, unpeeled
1/3 cup chopped scallions, green and white parts
1 English cucumber, sliced lengthwise, and then sliced across

1/2 cup chopped fresh dill
2/3 cup olive oil
4 tbsp. white wine vinegar
1 tbsp. Dijon-style mustard
Sea salt and freshly ground black pepper

Roughly chop the unpeeled potatoes and then boil them in a large pan of salted water until tender. Drain and cool. In a large bowl, combine the potatoes, scallions, cucumber slices, and dill.

In a separate small bowl, mix together the olive oil, vinegar, and mustard. Pour this dressing over the potato mixture. Season with salt and pepper. Toss until the salad is thoroughly mixed. Store in the refrigerator in an airtight container until needed.

Serves 6

picnic-style potato salad

see variations page 249

Remove this salad from the refrigerator an hour or two before serving to allow the flavors to return to life.

3 lbs. red-skinned potatoes
1 cup diced celery
1/2 cup diced, seeded cucumber
1/2 cup sliced green onions
1 1/4 cups Miracle Whip salad dressing
1 tbsp. prepared yellow mustard

1 tbsp. sugar
1 tbsp. fresh lemon juice
1/2 cup grated sharp cheddar cheese
3 hard-cooked eggs, diced
Sea salt and cracked black pepper to taste

Cut small red potatoes in half, large ones in quarters. Place in a large saucepan and cover with water. Bring to a boil and cook until tender, about 14 to 20 minutes. Drain and chill. Toss the potatoes in a large bowl with the celery, diced cucumber, and onions. Blend the Miracle Whip, mustard, sugar, lemon juice, cheese, eggs, salt, and pepper. Toss with the potato mixture. Cover and chill for at least 4 hours or overnight to blend the flavors.

Serves 6

barbecued corn

see variations page 250

Here's the classic barbecue vegetable.

8 ears of corn with husks
3 tbsp. butter
1 tsp. chili powder

1 tsp. onion salt
Freshly ground black pepper to taste

Pull the husks carefully from the corn so that each husk remains attached to the bottom of the ear. Remove any silk from the corn.

Melt the butter in a small saucepan, add the seasonings, and stir. Brush this butter mixture onto each ear of corn. Pull the corn husk up to cover the corn and wrap each piece in a sheet of heavy-duty foil.

Grill the corn directly over a medium-hot charcoal fire. Cook for 30 to 40 minutes, turning every few minutes. Carefully remove the foil and husk before serving.

Makes 8

spanish coleslaw

see variations page 251

This is sharper and lighter than the classic coleslaw, because it omits the typical mayonnaise dressing.

5 cups shredded green cabbage
1 cup shredded red cabbage
1/2 cup diced sweet red pepper or pimiento
1/4 cup diced green bell pepper
1/3 cup white wine vinegar
1/4 cup canola oil

3 tbsp. finely chopped onion
2 tbsp. sugar
1 tsp. celery salt
1 tsp. dry mustard
Sea salt and freshly ground black pepper

In a large bowl, combine the cabbages, red pepper, and green pepper. Place the remaining ingredients in a small jar with a tight-fitting lid. Screw on the lid and shake well to combine. Pour the dressing over the cabbage mixture just before serving and toss to coat. Serve with a slotted spoon.

Serves 6

garlic bread

see variations page 252

Another way to cook garlic bread is to grill the unbuttered and unsliced bread for about 2 minutes, brush with butter mixture, grill for 1 to 2 minutes more, and serve it cut into 2-inch slices.

1 loaf Italian or French bread
1/2 cup soft butter
2 pressed large cloves garlic
1 tsp. dried parsley flakes

1/4 tsp. crumbled dried oregano
1/4 tsp. dried dill
Grated Parmesan cheese to taste
Dried parsley flakes for sprinkling

Cut the bread into 1-inch slices but do not cut all the way through. Blend the butter, garlic, parsley, oregano, and dill. Spread this mixture on both sides of the bread slices. Put the loaf back together on a large piece of aluminum foil. Shape foil around the loaf of bread. Twist the ends of the foil to seal, but leave the top open. Sprinkle the top liberally with cheese and additional parsley flakes. Place on the grill away from the heat and cook for 30 minutes to 1 hour, until lightly toasted. The timing depends on the temperature.

Serves 4

scalloped green beans

see variations page 253

This Thanksgiving classic is ideal to serve al fresco in warmer weather. It goes well with grilled meat and fish.

3 cups green beans (fresh, canned, or frozen)
2 tbsp. butter
3 tbsp. flour
1 cup milk
1 cup shredded sharp cheddar cheese
1 tbsp. prepared mustard

1/2 cup bean cooking liquid
1/8 tsp. ground black pepper
1/2 tsp. salt
1/4 cup breadcrumbs tossed with 1 tbsp.
    melted butter

Top and tail the beans, and boil them in salted water until tender. Drain the beans and reserve 1/2 cup of the cooking liquid.

Melt 2 tablespoons butter in a saucepan and whisk in the flour. Add the milk slowly and cook over a low heat until thickened, stirring constantly. Add the cheese, mustard, and reserved cooking liquid to the pan. Stir constantly until the cheese melts. Add the salt and pepper. Place alternating layers of green beans and sauce in a greased casserole, then top with the buttered crumbs. Bake at 350°F (180°C) for 30 minutes and serve hot.

Serves 4

baked beans

see variations page 254

With the addition of meat and vegetables, these beans become a meal in a bowl.

1 lb. sliced bacon, diced
1/2 cup peeled and diced onion
1/2 cup diced green bell pepper

Two 15-oz. cans pork and beans
1 cup barbecue sauce
1 cup light brown sugar

In a large skillet, fry the bacon until tender-crisp. Drain on paper towel. Add the onion and green pepper to the reserved fat in the skillet and cook until soft. Drain to remove excess grease. Empty the beans into a casserole dish or bean pot, and add the bacon, onions, pepper, barbecue sauce, and sugar. Stir to combine. Bake at 350°F (180°C) for 45 minutes. Serve hot or, if preferred, at room temperature.

Serves 4

caribbean pinto beans

see variations page 255

Mottled pink pinto beans cook to a creamy texture that makes this dish perfect comfort food. It's an ideal way of using up leftover barbecued meat, too.

2 tbsp. olive oil
1 cup peeled and diced Spanish onion
1/2 cup diced sweet red bell pepper
2 cloves garlic, crushed
1 lb. dried pinto beans, rinsed and cleaned

1/2 cup water
2 tsp. salt
2 tsp. finely ground black pepper
1 tsp. ground allspice
2 cups barbecued pork scraps or burnt ends
1 cup barbecue sauce

Warm the oil in a skillet over medium-high heat and add the onion, pepper, and garlic. Sauté until just soft (about 5 minutes).

Combine the beans, onion, pepper, garlic, and water in a stockpot and bring to a boil. Reduce heat to a steady simmer over low, stirring occasionally, making sure that you don't scorch them. Cook until soft and heated through, about 30 to 45 minutes. Add the salt, pepper, and allspice. Stir in the meat and barbecue sauce. Simmer until the beans are soft and milky, about 10 more minutes.

Serves 6

garlic and dill grilled potatoes

see variations page 256

Plain baked potatoes are standard, clichéd barbecue fare — this recipe takes the dish to another level.

6 large potatoes, peeled and sliced
1 onion, halved and sliced
3 cloves garlic, pressed
1 tbsp. chopped fresh dill
3 tbsp. unsalted butter

1 cup shredded Monterey Jack cheese
Sea salt and freshly ground black pepper
    to taste

Preheat the grill. Place the potatoes, topped with the onion, garlic, dill, and butter, on a large sheet of heavy-duty aluminum foil. Seal the potatoes in the foil and place on the grill. Cook for 20 minutes on high heat. Turn the foil packet over once during the cooking process.

In the last 5 minutes of cooking, open the foil and sprinkle the potatoes with Monterey Jack. Reseal foil and cook for an additional 5 to 7 minutes. Before serving, season with salt and pepper.

Serves 6

creamy coleslaw

see variations page 257

Coleslaw has been a popular side dish since the days of ancient Rome. This version is especially appealing because the red cabbage lifts the otherwise muted colors.

1 cup mayonnaise
3 tbsp. sugar
2 tbsp. white wine vinegar
1/3 cup vegetable oil
1/4 tsp. onion powder
1/4 tsp. dry mustard
1/4 tsp. celery salt
1 tbsp. fresh lemon juice

1/2 cup half-and-half
Sea salt and freshly ground black pepper
6 cups finely shredded green cabbage
1/2 cup finely shredded red cabbage
1/4 cup peeled and diced onion
1/4 cup thinly sliced celery
1 carrot, grated

Blend the mayonnaise, sugar, vinegar, and oil. Add the onion powder, dry mustard, celery salt, lemon juice, half-and-half, salt, and pepper. Stir until smooth. Pour the coleslaw dressing over the shredded cabbage, onion, celery, and carrot in a large bowl. Toss until the vegetables are well coated. Keep the coleslaw refrigerated.

Serves 6

variations

potato salad with cucumber and dill

see base recipe page 231

yukon gold potato salad with tasso
Use Yukon gold potatoes in place of red potatoes. Replace the cucumber, scallions, dill, and dressing with a mixture of 1/2 cup vegetable oil; 1/4 cup each of cider vinegar, Creole mustard, and Dijon mustard; 2 tablespoons Worcestershire sauce; 1/2 teaspoon cayenne pepper; and 1/2 cup each of chopped Tasso or ham, diced onion, and chopped celery.

blue cheese and walnut potato salad
Instead of the cucumber, scallions, dill, and dressing, mix the following into the salad bowl: 1/2 cup toasted chopped walnuts; 1/4 cup each of milk, finely chopped fresh parsley, and crumbled blue cheese; 1 cup sour cream; 1 tablespoon sugar; and 1/2 teaspoon dry mustard.

sicilian potato salad
Instead of the cucumber, dressing, and dill, mix the following into the salad: 1/4 cup each of red wine vinegar, chopped flat-leaf parsley, and pitted chopped black olives; 4 tablespoons capers; 7 ounces extra-virgin olive oil; 2 tablespoons each of balsamic vinegar and fresh oregano; 1 tablespoon each of chopped anchovies, minced garlic, and salt; and 1/4 teaspoon chili flakes.

louisiana-style potato salad
Replace the dressing, dill, and cucumber with 5 cooked and crumbled slices bacon, 3/4 cup cream cheese dip, 1 tablespoon Louisiana hot sauce, 1/2 cup each of sliced green onions and sweet pickle relish, and 1/4 diced green bell pepper.

variations

picnic-style potato salad

see base recipe page 232

american potato salad with hard-boiled eggs and sweet pickles
Replace the celery, diced cucumber, scallion, and dressing with the following, whisked together: 1/4 cup each of red wine vinegar, chopped red onion, and sweet pickles; 1 cup mayonnaise; and 2 tablespoons each of Dijon mustard and chopped fresh parsley leaves.

jalapeño potato salad
Replace the dressing with the following, whisked together: 1/2 cup extra-virgin olive oil and 1/4 cup each of mayonnaise and Dijon mustard. Mix into the salad 1/4 cup sliced green onions, 1/4 cup crumbled feta cheese, 4 seeded and minced jalapeños, 2 tablespoons white wine vinegar, and 2 pressed cloves garlic.

sweet potato-apple salad
Replace the potatoes with 3 pounds sweet potatoes. Omit the celery, cucumber, and scallions. Instead of the picnic-style dressing, mix the potatoes with 1 apple, cored and diced; 1/2 cup each of chopped pecans, sour cream, and mayonnaise; 1 teaspoon grated lemon zest; 2 tablespoons each of fresh lemon juice and honey; and 1/4 teaspoon dried tarragon.

jamaican potato salad
Omit the diced cucumber. Replace with 4 thick slices bacon, cooked and crumbled; 1 1/4 cups mayonnaise; 1 tablespoon each of dry mustard and fresh thyme; 1/2 teaspoon each of ground allspice and turmeric; pinch of cayenne pepper; 6 diced cornichons; 1/4 cup each of chopped celery and onion; and 2 teaspoons Louisiana hot sauce.

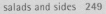

variations

barbecued corn

see base recipe page 235

grilled corn italian-style
Replace the butter, chili powder, onion salt, and pepper with a mixture of 1/4 cup olive oil, 1 teaspoon Italian seasoning, and sea salt and cracked black pepper to taste.

corn on the cob with spicy lime butter
Omit the butter, chili powder, salt, and pepper. Make a flavored butter to serve with the corn: blend together 8 tablespoons unsalted butter, softened, grated zest of 1 lime, 1 canned chipotle chili with adobo sauce, and salt to taste. Chill. Grill corn as in the base recipe, serving a disc of the butter on top of each grilled ear so that it melts into the corn.

cajun-grilled corn on the cob
Prepare the base recipe. Roll the grilled corn in a rub made from 1 teaspoon each of dried oregano and paprika; 3/4 teaspoon each of garlic and onion powder; 1/2 teaspoon salt; 1/4 teaspoon dried thyme and black pepper; and 1/8 teaspoon cayenne.

grilled wino corn on the cob
Prepare the corn as in the base recipe but do not wrap the ears in aluminum foil. Baste the corn while grilling with a mixture of 5 tablespoons melted butter and 1/2 cup red wine.

cumin grilled corn
Replace the chili powder and onion salt with 1 1/2 teaspoons ground cumin, 1/2 teaspoon salt, and 1/2 teaspoon turmeric. Proceed with the base recipe.

variations

spanish coleslaw

see base recipe page 236

cabbage and corn slaw
Omit the celery salt and dry mustard. Add to the base recipe 2 cups cooked corn, 1/2 cup diced red onions, 1/4 cup diced yellow pepper, 1 to 2 tablespoons seeded and chopped jalapeño pepper, 1/4 cup sugar, 1/3 cup each of white vinegar and canola oil, and 1/2 teaspoon freshly ground black pepper.

sweet and sassy vanilla slaw
Replace the cabbage with 5 cups shredded and chopped Napa or Chinese cabbage. In place of the peppers, use 8 ounces chopped raw broccoli stems and 8 ounces peeled and grated carrot. Omit the mustard and celery salt from the dressing and replace them with 1/3 cup sugar, 2 teaspoons vanilla extract, 1/2 teaspoon ground ginger, and 1/4 teaspoon cayenne.

mango jicama slaw
Replace the cabbage and peppers with 1 mango, 1 red bell pepper, and 1 pound jicama, all peeled and cut into julienne, and 1 large jalapeño, seeded and minced. Omit the celery salt, vinegar, and mustard from the dressing and replace them with 1/2 cup fresh lime juice and 2 tablespoons each of fresh chopped cilantro and parsley.

carolina slaw
Replace the peppers with 1/4 cup chopped sweet onions and 2 grated carrots. In place of the dressing, in a saucepan 2/3 cup sugar, 1 teaspoon salt, 1/3 cup vegetable oil, 1 teaspoon celery seeds, and 2/3 cup cider vinegar. Bring to a boil, let cool, and pour over vegetables.

variations

garlic bread

see base recipe page 239

parsley-garlic bread
Replace the oregano and dill with 2 additional tablespoons parsley flakes and 1/4 teaspoon ground red pepper (optional).

provolone-garlic bread
Replace the parsley, oregano, dill, and Parmesan with 1 teaspoon Worcestershire sauce and 1/2 pound grated provolone cheese.

most delicious garlic-cheese bread
Replace the butter, parsley, oregano, and dill with a mixture of 4 tablespoons olive oil, 2 additional pressed large cloves garlic, 3/4 cup mayonnaise, and 1 cup grated Parmesan. Omit the Parmesan cheese sprinkled on top in the base recipe.

go-go garlic bread
Replace the dill with 1/2 cup mayonnaise, 1 tablespoon grated Parmesan, 1/4 teaspoon dried basil, 1/4 teaspoon seasoning salt, and 1/2 cup shredded Monterey Jack cheese.

gremolata garlic bread
Replace the oregano and dill with 1 1/2 teaspoons grated lemon rind. Increase the quantity of dried parsley flakes in the flavored butter to 2 teaspoons.

variations

scalloped green beans

see base recipe page 240

green bean casserole
Replace the cheese sauce with a 10 3/4-ounce can condensed cream of mushroom soup. Top the finished casserole with 1 1/3 cups canned French Fried Onions instead of the breadcrumbs.

creamy green bean casserole
Replace the cheese sauce with a sauce made of 8 ounces cream cheese at room temperature, 1/2 cup milk, 2 tablespoons dry ranch-style salad dressing mix, 1/4 teaspoon white pepper, 1 cup diced onion, 2 pressed cloves garlic, 1 1/2 cups sliced fresh mushrooms, and 3/4 cup breadcrumbs.

holiday green beans
Replace the cheese sauce with a mixture of 1/4 cup each of heavy cream, chopped mushrooms, toasted walnuts, and coarsely chopped scallions; and garlic salt to taste. Instead of the breadcrumbs, top with 4 slices bacon, cooked and crumbled.

green bean casserole with tomatoes and mozzarella
Replace the cheese sauce with a mixture of 2 plum tomatoes, seeded and diced; 8 ounces shredded mozzarella; 1/4 cup chopped onion; and 1/2 cup each of heavy cream and sour cream. Instead of the breadcrumbs, top with 1 cup crushed ranch-flavored potato chips.

variations

baked beans

see base recipe page 243

apple baked beans
Replace the bacon, sugar, onion, pepper, and barbecue sauce with 1 cup apple juice;
1 teaspoon salt; 1 teaspoon dry mustard; 1/2 pound cooked and diced bacon; 1/2 cup
molasses; 1/2 cup diced celery; and 2 cups crisp apples, peeled, cored, and chopped.

peachy baked beans
Replace the bacon and pepper with a 16-ounce can peach pie filling, 1/2 cup diced sweet
red pepper, 1 teaspoon sea salt, and freshly ground black pepper to taste.

pineapple-bourbon baked beans
Replace the bacon, sugar, onion, pepper, and barbecue sauce with 1 teaspoon dry mustard;
1 cup chili sauce; 1 cup crushed pineapple, drained; 2 tablespoons molasses; 1/4 cup
good-quality bourbon; and 1/2 cup strong coffee.

cola baked beans
Replace the bacon, onion, pepper, sugar, and barbecue sauce with a 12-ounce can cola.

cherry cola baked beans
Replace the bacon, onion, pepper, sugar, and barbecue sauce with a 12-ounce can cherry
cola. Add 1/4 cup pitted cherries to the beans.

variations

caribbean pinto beans

see base recipe page 244

beans and greens
Replace the bell pepper, barbecued meat, and sauce with 1 pound sliced smoked sausage, 16 ounces frozen chopped turnip greens with diced turnips, and 1 teaspoon crushed red pepper flakes. Proceed with the base recipe.

hard rock café barbecued beans
Replace the vegetables, oil, meat, flavorings, and sauce with 2 tablespoons water, 2 tablespoons cornstarch, 1/2 cup ketchup, 1/4 cup each of white vinegar and light brown sugar, 2 tablespoons diced onion, 1 teaspoon prepared mustard, 1/2 teaspoon chili powder, 1/4 teaspoon each of salt and coarse ground black pepper, and 1/2 cup cooked bacon. Proceed with the base recipe.

barbecued cowboy pinto beans
Replace the bell pepper and barbecued meat with 1 tablespoon chili powder, 1/2 cup ketchup, 2 tablespoons prepared yellow mustard, and a dash of Tabasco sauce. Proceed with the base recipe.

el paso border beans
Replace the bell pepper, meat, and sauce with 2 tablespoons lard or vegetable oil; 5 slices bacon, cooked and chopped; 3/4 cup cooked and chopped chorizo; 1 pound tomatoes, peeled, seeded and chopped; 6 serrano chilies, chopped; and 1 teaspoon ground cumin. Proceed with the base recipe.

variations

garlic and dill grilled potatoes

see base recipe page 246

baked potatoes on the grill
Replace the onions, cheese, garlic, butter, and dill with 5 tablespoons melted unsalted butter, 4 thinly sliced green onions, and 1 cup sliced medium button mushrooms.

roasted potato packages
Replace the cheese, garlic, butter, and dill with 1 green pepper, cut into strips; 4 tablespoons olive oil; 4 tablespoons balsamic vinegar; and lemon pepper to taste.

grilled potato and onion packages
Replace the cheese, garlic, butter, and dill with 2/3 cup olive oil; 1 tablespoon Dijon mustard; 2 tablespoons chopped fresh thyme; and 2 large red onions, halved and sliced 1/2-inch thick. Garnish cooked potatoes with sprigs of fresh thyme.

grilled garlic potatoes with corn
Replace the onions, cheese, garlic, and dill with 2 cups corn kernels. Make a dressing by whisking together 6 roasted large garlic cloves; 4 tablespoons olive oil; 1 tablespoon each of finely chopped fresh rosemary, white wine vinegar, and Dijon mustard; and 2 thinly sliced green onions.

variations

creamy coleslaw

see base recipe page 247

southern coleslaw
Replace the red cabbage and dressing with 1/2 cup diced sweet red pepper, 1 teaspoon celery seeds, and 1/4 cup mayonnaise, and mix. Combine in saucepan 1 cup water, 3 tablespoons white vinegar, and 2 tablespoons sugar. Bring to a boil and pour over the slaw.

honey deli-style coleslaw
Omit the red cabbage. Replace the dressing with the following ingredients, stirred together to blend: 1/2 cup clover honey, 1 teaspoon whole celery seeds, and 1/2 cup each of sour cream and mayonnaise.

coleslaw with creamy tangy dressing
Omit the red cabbage. Replace the dressing with the following ingredients, stirred together: 1 1/4 cups mayonnaise, 1/3 cup sugar, 1/4 cup white wine vinegar, and 1/4 teaspoon celery seeds.

cabbage slaw with apple and raisins
Replace the red cabbage and onion with 2 cups unpeeled, cored, and diced apples and 1/2 cup raisins. Omit the dressing and replace with 1 1/2 cups Miracle Whip salad dressing.

sweet sizzlers

A surprising range of sweet treats can be cooked up on a grill, and this chapter shows you how. It also contains desserts prepared in other ways, which are great at the end of a barbecue to round things off in style.

peach cobbler

see variations page 273

Especially good topped with a scoop of homemade vanilla ice cream, this is a wonderful way to finish a barbecue supper.

4 1/2 cups sliced and peeled peaches	1/4 cup sugar
1/2 cup sugar (more if desired)	1 1/2 tsp. baking powder
2 tbsp. fresh lemon juice	1/2 tsp. baking soda
1 tsp. pure vanilla	1/4 tsp. salt
1/2 tsp. ground ginger	1/4 cup unsalted butter, chilled and cubed
1/4 tsp. freshly grated nutmeg	2/3 cup buttermilk
1 1/3 cups all-purpose flour	Additional sugar to sprinkle on top

Combine the first 6 ingredients (peaches through nutmeg). Spoon the peach mixture into a greased shallow 2-quart baking dish. Cover with foil and bake at 400°F (200°C) for 15 minutes or until the peach mixture is hot and bubbly.

Meanwhile, to prepare the biscuit topping, combine the flour, 1/4 cup sugar, baking powder, soda, and salt in a bowl. Cut in the butter with a pastry knife until the mixture resembles coarse crumbs. Add the buttermilk and stir just until combined. Remove the dish from the oven and uncover. Drop 1/4 cup measures of dough evenly on top of the peach mixture. Lightly sprinkle additional sugar over the dough. Continue baking, uncovered, for 30 minutes or until the biscuits are golden and a cake tester inserted in the center of the biscuits comes out clean. Serve warm with cream or ice cream.

Serves 4

summer fruit packets

see variations page 274

Fresh mint adds a wonderful depth of flavor to fruit, especially when the flavor is enhanced with sugar and citrus. Next time you make a fruit salad, add some finely chopped fresh mint for a little extra zing.

2 peaches
Boiling water
1/2 lb. strawberries, hulled and washed
1/2 lb. cherries, pitted
2 kiwifruit, peeled and sliced

4 tbsp. unsalted butter
2 tbsp. packed brown sugar
Grated zest and juice of 1 orange
4 sprigs fresh mint

Place the peaches in a bowl and pour boiling water over them. Let stand for 1 minute, then drain and peel. Cut the peaches in half, remove their pits, and slice. Put the cherries and strawberries in a large bowl and add the sliced peaches and kiwifruit. Gently mix.

Cut 4 large squares of heavy-duty foil. Divide the fruit between the squares. Heat the butter, sugar, orange zest, and orange juice over medium heat in a small saucepan until the sugar has melted. Spoon this mixture over the fruit and top each portion with a sprig of mint. Close the packets, being sure to secure the seams.

Grill the packets over medium heat for about 10 minutes. Serve with whipped cream or ice cream.

Serves 4

texas sheet cake with chocolate frosting

see variations page 275

This rich cake with its sumptuously sweet frosting is an American classic.

One 18 1/4-oz. chocolate cake mix
1 cup buttermilk
1/3 cup unsalted butter, melted
2 large eggs, lightly beaten
1 tsp. vanilla extract
for chocolate frosting
1/4 cup milk, plus 2 tbsp.

1/4 cup cocoa powder
1/2 cup butter, softened
1 lb. confectioners' sugar, sifted (about 4 cups)
1 tsp. vanilla extract
1 cup toasted chopped pecans

Beat together the first 5 ingredients with an electric mixer at full speed for 2 minutes or until blended. Pour into a greased and floured 13 x 9 x 2-inch baking pan. Bake at 350°F (180°C) for 15 to 20 minutes or until a wooden toothpick inserted in the middle comes out clean.

Meanwhile, prepare the frosting. Start by mixing the milk and cocoa powder in a heavy saucepan. Add the butter and, over medium heat, stir until it melts. Remove from the heat and gradually stir in the sugar and vanilla until smooth. Add the pecans.

When the cake is just out of the oven, spread the frosting evenly on the hot cake. Let cool before serving.

Serves 6

grandma's fried fruit pies

see variations page 276

No fruit pie will ever taste as good as my grandma's. Luckily she left me the recipe so I can pass it on to you.

3 cups all-purpose flour
1 tsp. salt
3/4 cup vegetable shortening
1 egg, lightly beaten
1/4 cup cold water
1 tsp. white vinegar
21-oz. can peach pie filling

Mix together the flour and salt. Cut in the shortening with a fork until the mixture resembles coarse crumbs. Stir together the beaten egg and the water, and sprinkle over the flour mixture. Sprinkle in the vinegar and mix lightly, until the ingredients are well combined. Form the dough into a ball and wrap in plastic wrap. Refrigerate for at least one hour.

Roll the dough thin. Cut into 2 1/2- to 3-inch squares. Divide the filling between each square, piling it up in the middle of the pastry. Press the edges together to form a triangle. Let the pies stand for a few minutes before frying.

Two methods of frying: deep-fry, at 375°F (190°C) for 3 to 4 minutes; or pan-fry the pies in about 1/2-inch of oil in an electric frying pan set to 375°F (190°C) for 5 to 6 minutes. In both cases, fry in hot vegetable oil until golden brown. Remove from the fat and drain. Sprinkle the hot pies with confectioners' sugar or cinnamon sugar.

Serves 6–8

grilled s'mores

see variations page 277

North America's favorite fireside treat normally uses graham crackers—here's my own tortilla version.

Flour tortilla shells
1 jar peanut butter
1 bag miniature chocolate chips
1 bag miniature marshmallows

Spread peanut butter on half of the tortilla shells. Sprinkle those tortillas with chocolate chips and marshmallows. Grill the plain and filled tortillas at the same time, for about 3 to 4 minutes. Flip a plain tortilla on top of each filled one. Cut into wedges and serve.

Alternatively, roll the filled tortillas up like a burrito and wrap each one in heavy-duty foil. Seal the ends by folding over the tinfoil. Put on the edge of the fire or above the coals until heated through, then unwrap and enjoy.

Serves 4–6

grilled pineapple with molasses-lime butter

see variations page 278

This sweet butter is the perfect partner for soft, ripe pineapple slices.

1 ripe pineapple, peeled, cored, top and bottom removed
Vegetable oil
Salt and freshly ground black pepper to taste

1/4 cup molasses
1/4 cup butter
2 tbsp. fresh lime juice

Cut the pineapple crosswise into 6 slices, each about 1 inch thick. Brush the cut surfaces of the pineapple slices lightly with oil; sprinkle with salt and pepper. Grill over medium coals for about 8 to 10 minutes, until golden brown. Turn and grill the other side to brown it. Meanwhile, combine the molasses, butter, and lime juice in a small saucepan, and stir together over low heat until the butter is melted. Remove the pineapple slices from the grill, brush with molasses-lime butter, and serve.

Serves 6

glazed pears

see variations page 279

Spooning a wine-based syrup over pears before grilling makes the fruit taste delectable.

6 large pears
Grated zest and juice of 1/2 lemon
4 tbsp. maple syrup
1 tsp. vanilla extract
4 tbsp. red wine
3 tbsp. chopped pistachio nuts

Peel, core, and halve the pears. Cut 6 squares of heavy-duty foil and lay a halved pear on each piece of foil. Combine the remaining ingredients except the pistachios in a small saucepan and heat to boiling point. Remove from the heat and spoon the mixture over each pear. Close the foil packets, being sure to secure the seams.

Grill the pears for 5 to 8 minutes over medium heat, until they are hot and tender but retain their shape. Open each packet and brush or spoon the juices from the packet back over the fruit. Sprinkle a few chopped pistachio nuts over each portion and serve.

Serves 6

peaches with blue cheese and honey

see variations page 280

Blue cheese isn't often used in desserts — but its rich creaminess is essential here.

6 ripe peaches, halved and pitted
2 tbsp. vegetable oil
12 tsp. Maytag blue cheese or mascarpone
12 tsp. honey, preferably clover

Black pepper to taste
Fresh mint leaves or sprigs for garnish

Brush the cut sides of the peaches with oil and place on a grill preheated to medium, cut-side down. Grill until caramelized. Turn over and grill until almost soft, about 1 to 2 minutes more.

Transfer the peaches to a platter, cut-sides up, and place a spoonful of cheese in the center of each. Drizzle with honey and grind fresh pepper to taste over the peaches. Garnish with mint and serve.

Serves 6

homemade vanilla ice cream

see variations page 281

No store-bought ice cream tastes as good as homemade; and this version is particularly appealing, without any tricky custard-making or constant stirring.

4 cups half-and-half or light cream
14-oz. can sweetened condensed milk
1/2 cup superfine sugar
1 tbsp. vanilla extract

2 cups whipping cream (for refrigerator-freezer method only)

In a 2-quart ice cream maker container, combine all the ingredients and mix well. Freeze according to the manufacturer's instructions; this should take about 40 minutes.

Alternatively, try the refrigerator-freezer method. Omit the half-and-half. In a large bowl, combine the sweetened condensed milk and vanilla. Fold in 2 cups whipping cream, whipped. Pour into a 9 x 5-inch loaf pan or another 2-quart container. Cover and freeze for 6 hours or until firm.

Serves 4–6

variations

peach cobbler

see base recipe page 259

blueberry cobbler
Replace the peaches and lemon juice with 5 cups blueberries, 1/2 cup sugar, and 1/3 cup water. Use 1 tablespoon ground cinnamon in place of the ginger.

peach-berry cobbler
Reduce the quantity of peaches to 2 1/2 cups. Omit the lemon juice and ginger. Add 2 cups berries and 1 1/2 additional cups sugar.

blackberry cobbler
Replace the peaches and lemon juice with 5 cups blackberries, 3/4 cup sugar, 3 tablespoons cornstarch, and 2 tablespoons unsalted butter.

sour cherry cobbler
Replace the peaches and ginger with 6 cups pitted sour cherries, 1/2 cup water, 2/3 cup sugar, and 1 tablespoon cornstarch.

variations

summer fruit packets

see base recipe page 260

summer fruit packets with kirsch
Prepare the basic recipe, adding 1 tablespoon kirsch to each packet.

fruits of the forest packets
Prepare the basic recipe, replacing the peaches and kiwifruit with 1/2 pound raspberries and the same quantity of blueberries.

tropical fruit packets
Prepare the basic recipe, replacing the peaches, strawberries, and cherries with 1/2 pound pineapple chunks and 1/2 pound papaya chunks.

summer fruit packets with white wine
Prepare the basic recipe, adding 1 tablespoon white wine to each packet.

texas sheet cake with chocolate frosting

see base recipe page 263

blonde texas sheet cake with chocolate frosting
Replace the chocolate cake mix with an 18 1/4-ounce white cake mix.

lazy daisy sheet cake with buttermilk frosting
Make the cake as in the base recipe. Replace the frosting with 1 cup light brown sugar and 3 tablespoons buttermilk, combined in a bowl. Garnish with 1 cup toasted chopped pecans.

carrot sheet cake with cream cheese frosting
Replace the chocolate cake mix with an 18-ounce carrot cake mix. Make a cream cheese frosting by combining 1/4 cup softened butter; 11 ounces cream cheese, softened; and 1/2 teaspoon vanilla extract.

german chocolate sheet cake with chocolate coconut frosting
Replace the chocolate cake mix with an 18 1/4-ounce German chocolate cake mix. Prepare the frosting as in the base recipe, adding 1 1/2 cups toasted shredded coconut to the ingredients.

variations

grandma's fried fruit pies

see base recipe page 264

apple fried pies
Prepare the basic recipe, replacing the peach pie filling with a 21-ounce can apple pie filling.

cherry fried pies
Prepare the basic recipe, replacing the peach pie filling with a 21-ounce can cherry pie filling.

blueberry fried pies
Prepare the basic recipe, replacing the peach pie filling with a 21-ounce can blueberry
pie filling.

french apple fried pies
Prepare the basic recipe, replacing the peach pie filling with a 21-ounce can apple pie
filling combined with 2 tablespoons each of golden raisins and currants, 1 teaspoon ground
cinnamon, and 1 teaspoon grated lemon zest.

dried fruit fried pies
Prepare the basic recipe, replacing the peach pie filling with 3 cups mixed dried fruit such as
apples, apricots, pears, and peaches.

variations

grilled s'mores

see base recipe page 267

fluffy nutters
Replace the chocolate chips and marshmallows with 1 jar marshmallow cream.

open-faced cinnamon crisp
Replace the peanut butter, chocolate chips, and marshmallows with a cinnamon filling, made by combining 1/2 pound melted butter, 1/4 cup granulated sugar, and 1 tablespoon ground cinnamon. Do not place an unfilled tortilla over the top of each filled one.

open-faced mascarpone gorgonzola torte
Replace the peanut butter, chocolate chips, and marshmallows with 8 ounces mascarpone, 4 ounces crumbled gorgonzola, and 1/2 cup blueberries. Do not place an unfilled tortilla over the top of each filled one.

snickers delight dessert tortillas
Replace the peanut butter, marshmallows, and chocolate chips with 1 block of almond bark; 3 large Snickers candy bars, chopped up; and 1 bag sweetened shredded coconut.

variations

grilled pineapple with molasses-lime butter

see base recipe page 268

honeysuckle pineapple
Prepare the basic recipe, replacing the molasses, butter, and lime juice with a mixture of 1/4 cup clover honey, 2 tablespoons cherry brandy, and 1 tablespoon fresh lemon juice.

grilled sweet curried pineapple
Omit the molasses, butter, and lime juice. Instead rub the pineapple before grilling with a mixture of 1/4 cup packed dark brown sugar and 1/2 teaspoon curry powder or to taste. Grill the pineapple as in the base recipe. Pour 1/2 cup plain yogurt over the grilled pineapple and garnish with 3 tablespoons toasted coconut.

grilled piña colada
Omit the molasses, butter, and lime juice. Grill the pineapple as in the base recipe. Pour over the grilled fruit a sauce made by combining 1/4 cup canned coconut milk, 1 tablespoon light rum, 1/4 cup sugar, and 1 tablespoon ground cinnamon.

hot buttered rum pineapple
Omit the molasses and lime. Instead, flavor the melted butter with 1/4 cup brown sugar, 2 tablespoons dark rum, 1 tablespoon ground cinnamon, and 1/2 teaspoon each of ground ginger, nutmeg, and cloves. Grill the pineapple as in the base recipe.

glazed pears

see base recipe page 269

glazed pears with white wine syrup
Prepare the base recipe, replacing the red wine with white wine.

glazed pears with brandy syrup
Prepare the base recipe, replacing the red wine with brandy.

glazed pears with chocolate sauce
Prepare the base recipe, replacing the red wine with 2 ounces chocolate chips, divided
equally between the 6 foil packets.

moroccan-style glazed pears
Prepare the base recipe, omitting the wine and adding 2 drops orange-flower water and
2 drops rosewater to each packet.

variations

peaches with blue cheese and honey

see base recipe page 270

grilled peaches and cream
Replace the cheese and pepper with 2 tablespoons clover honey and 1 cup cream cheese.

sweet grilled glazed peaches
Replace the cheese and pepper with 1/2 cup honey and 2 tablespoons cinnamon.

grilled peaches with raspberry puree
Omit the cheese, honey, and pepper. Grill the peaches as in the base recipe, basting regularly with a glaze made by mixing 2 tablespoons brown sugar, 1/4 teaspoon ground cinnamon, 2 teaspoons Meyers rum, and 2 teaspoons melted unsalted butter. Serve the grilled peaches with a sauce made by combining 1/2 cup seedless raspberry jam and 2 teaspoons of fresh lemon juice.

grilled balsamic-glazed peaches
Omit the cheese and honey. Spread over the peach halves a glaze made by mixing 1/2 cup balsamic vinegar and 3 tablespoons light brown sugar. Proceed to grill as in the base recipe.

homemade vanilla ice cream

see base recipe page 272

peach ice cream
Omit 2 teaspoons of the vanilla. Prepare the ice cream as in the base recipe, flavoring it by stirring in 2 cups mashed peaches, 1 teaspoon almond extract, and a few drops each of yellow and red food coloring before freezing.

strawberry ice cream
Omit 2 teaspoons of the vanilla. Prepare the ice cream as in the base recipe, flavoring it by stirring in 2 cups mashed strawberries and a few drops of red food coloring before freezing.

banana ice cream
Omit 2 teaspoons of the vanilla. Prepare the ice cream as in the base recipe, mashing 4 ripe medium bananas and stirring them into the ice cream before freezing.

chocolate ice cream
Prepare the ice cream as in the base recipe, replacing the sugar, half-and-half, and vanilla with 2/3 cup chocolate sauce and 2 cups heavy cream.

index

Aïoli 71, 167
  basil aïoli 226
almond-cilantro pesto 188
anchovy sauce 76
andouille-stuffed jalapeños 45
angel's bruschetta 42
apple jelly:
  apple-glazed lamb chops 147
  apple-honey glazed chicken 109
apple pie filling:
  apple fried pies 276
  French apple fried pies 276
apples:
  apple baked beans 254
  apple-raisin stuffed chicken
    thighs 85
  cabbage slaw with apple and
    raisins 257
  sweet potato-apple salad 249
apricots:
  fruit and vegetable kabobs 227
armadillo eggs 45
artichokes:
  artichoke kebabs 44
  citrus artichokes 44
  grilled artichokes with lemon
    yogurt 44
  hitching post grilled artichokes 44
  marinated grilled artichokes 32
asparagus:
  asparagus with black pepper 208
  asparagus with honey-garlic
    sauce 224
  grilled asparagus with red onion
    and orange 224
  grilled asparagus with red pepper
    sauce 224
  grilled sesame asparagus 224
  grilled vegetable platter with
    balsamic maple dressing 212
avocado:
  grilled red snapper with soy sauce
    and avocado 75

Bacon:
  apple baked beans 254
  bacon and olive-stuffed
    mushrooms 34
  bacon wraps 23
  bacon-wrapped barbecued pork
    loin 146

bacon-wrapped dates 38
bacon-wrapped jalapeño
  poppers 33
bacon-wrapped pineapple
  chunks 38
bacon-wrapped shrimp 38
bacon-wrapped water chestnuts 38
baked beans 243
"bit" pizza appetizer 40
El Paso border beans 255
grilled southwestern bacon-
  wrapped beef tenderloin 187
bananas:
  banana ice cream 281
  fruit and vegetable kabobs 227
basil:
  basil aïoli 226
  fresh basil vinaigrette 226
  tomato-basil bruschetta 29
beans:
  apple baked beans 254
  baked beans 243
  barbecued cowboy pinto beans 255
  beans and greens 255
  Caribbean pinto beans 244
  cherry cola baked beans 254
  cola baked beans 254
  creamy green bean casserole 253
  El Paso border beans 255
  green bean casserole 253
    with tomatoes and
    mozzarella 253
  Hard Rock Café barbecued
    beans 255
  holiday green beans 253
  peachy baked beans 254
  pineapple-bourbon baked
    beans 254
  scalloped green beans 240
  veggie burgers 229
  zesty white bean burgers 229
béarnaise butter 168
beef:
  Amarillo Texas marinated skirt
    steak 194
  Argentinian-style rib eye
    steaks 174
  balsamic hanger steaks 163
  barbecued baby beef ribs 171
  barbecued chuck steak 192

barbecued short ribs 178
barbecued teriyaki meatballs 39
bbq sweet and spicy meatballs 24
beef brisket with spicy rub 153
beef ribs with Chinese spices 191
beef tenderloin with mustard
  tarragon cream sauce 187
beer-marinated peppered
  t-bones 161
Bichelmeyer's meat market
  fajitas 181
Big Bill's beef ribs 191
Big Billy's cowboy rib eye
  steaks 193
Cajun-style rib eye steak 193
Caribbean jerk beef steak 188
carne asada 154
chuck pepper steak 192
coffee bean and gourmet
  peppercorn crusted steak 190
company-coming t-bones 184
deviled chuck steak 172
French bistro burger 183
grilled beef tenderloin 187
grilled Chilean skirt steaks 175
grilled flank steak with aïoli 167
grilled flank steak with almond-
  cilantro pesto 188
grilled flank steak with
  nectarines 188
grilled garlic skirt steak 194
grilled hanger steaks 186
grilled Korean short ribs 196
grilled marinated sirloin steak 162
grilled rib eye steaks with creamed
  mushrooms 193
grilled southwestern bacon-
  wrapped beef tenderloin 187
grilled steaks with martini
  twist 185
grilled t-bones with cowboy grilled
  onions 184
grilled Texas beef short ribs 196
grilled tri-tip roast 179
hamburgers with "hot" barbecue
  sauce 183
hanger steaks with mustard jus 186
hanger steaks with shallots 186
herbed hanger steaks 186
Jack's barbecued sweet beef ribs 191

Jack's brisket rub 180
Korean bulgogi 185
mango strip steak 190
Manuel's fajitas 181
marinated grilled porterhouse 182
marinated tri-tip 197
New Mexico green chili burgers 183
New Mexico grilled skirt steak 194
Oriental barbecued chuck steak 192
pale ale porterhouse 157
peppered steak with tarragon 185
perfect strip steak 190
porterhouse steaks with bourbon
  and shallot sauce 182
porterhouse steaks with mushroom
  and garlic sauce 182
red wine short ribs 196
Rib Doctor rib eye steaks 193
Romanian beef tenderloin 187
Santa Fe flank steak 188
Santa Maria-style grilled
  tri-tip 197
smoked Italian meatballs 39
smoky cocktail meatballs 39
Southern grilled garlic
  porterhouse 182
spicy grilled beef tri-trip 197
spicy grilled skirt steak 194
spicy Kansas City brisket rub 180
spicy Kansas City grilled beef short
  ribs 196
spiky lime carne asada 181
steak au poivre rouge 190
steak and baby portobellos 185
steak quesadillas 41
strip steak simple 169
Stu Carpenter's brisket rub 180
Stu's barbecued chuck steak 192
t-bone à la blue 184
t-bones and wild mushroom
  medley 184
tasty tequila tri-tip 197
tender smoked beef ribs 191
tenderloin with herbed cheese 164
Texas brisket rub 180
ultimate steakhouse burger 158
West Texas grilled fajitas 181
beer:
  beer and cayenne grilled
    onions 219

beer and herb shrimp 62
beer-marinated peppered
    t-bones 161
herbed beer can chicken 82
pale ale porterhouse 157
root beer can chicken
    barbecue 103
stout beer can chicken
    barbecue 103
sweet California beer can chicken
    barbecue 103
bell peppers see peppers
berries:
    peach-berry cobbler 273
    blackberry cobbler 273
blueberries:
    blueberry cobbler 273
    fruits of the forest packets 274
    open-faced mascarpone gorgonzola
        torte 277
    blueberry fried pies 276
bourbon:
    bourbon pork tenderloins 141
    bourbon and shallot sauce 182
    pineapple-bourbon baked
        beans 254
brandy:
    glazed pears with brandy syrup 279
brat burgers 139
bread:
    garlic bread 239
    go-go garlic bread 252
    gremolata garlic bread 252
    most delicious garlic cheese
        bread 252
    parsley-garlic bread 252
    provolone-garlic bread 252
broccoli:
    sweet and sassy vanilla slaw 251
bruschetta:
    angel's bruschetta 42
    bruschetta with roasted peppers 42
    cheesy bruschetta 42
    shrimp bruschetta 42
    tomato-basil bruschetta 29
buffalo sauce 35
burgers:
    brat burgers 139
    Grape-Nut burgers 218

hamburgers with "hot" barbecue
    sauce 183
healthy grilled burgers 189
herbed pork burgers 139
New Mexico green chili
    burgers 183
New Orleans andouille burgers 139
teriyaki pork burgers 115
veggie burgers 229
zesty white bean burgers 229
butter:
    béarnaise butter 168
    blue cheese, rosemary, and balsamic
        vinegar butter 189
    chipotle-chili steak butter 189
    garlic butter 73
    garlic-herb butter 12
    maître d'hôtel butter (king of steak
        butters) 189
    molasses butter 120
    molasses-lime butter 268
    pesto-walnut butter 189
    shallot butter 75
    spicy lime butter 250
buttermilk:
    buttermilk frosting 275
    grilled buttermilk turkey
        drumsticks 113

Cabbage:
    cabbage slaw with apple and
        raisins 257
    coleslaw with creamy tangy
        dressing 257
    creamy coleslaw 247
    honey deli-style coleslaw 257
    Spanish coleslaw 236
    sweet and sassy vanilla slaw 251
cabrito see goat
cakes:
    blonde Texas sheet cake with
        chocolate frosting 275
    carrot sheet cake with cream
        cheese frosting 275
    German chocolate sheet cake with
        chocolate coconut frosting 275
    lazy daisy sheet cake with
        buttermilk frosting 275
    Texas sheet cake with chocolate
        frosting 263

carne asada 154
    spiky lime carne asada 181
carrot sheet cake wtih cream cheese
    frosting 275
carrots:
    Carolina slaw 251
    grilled vegetable platter with
        balsamic maple dressing 212
catfish:
    barbecued catfish 79
    Creole-grilled catfish 79
    grilled catfish 66
    grilled smoky catfish 79
celery:
    apple baked beans 254
    creamy coleslaw 247
    picnic-style potato salad 232
    vegetable kabobs 215
    Yukon gold potato salad with
        Tasso 248
    char siu Chinese barbecued
        pork 145
cheese:
    blue cheese sauce 142
    blue cheese and walnut potato
        salad 248
    blue cheese-stuffed mushrooms 34
    blue cheese, rosemary, and balsamic
        vinegar butter 189
    cheesy bruschetta 42
    cream cheese frosting 275
    green bean casserole with tomatoes
        and mozzarella 253
    grilled blue cheese halibut 73
    grilled pizza 26
    grilled quesadillas 27
    grilled squash parmesan 225
    Italian pizza with goat cheese 40
    most delicious garlic-cheese
        bread 252
    open-faced mascarpone gorgonzola
        torte 277
    peaches with blue cheese and
        honey 270
    provolone-garlic bread 252
    stuffed Monterey mushrooms 15
    t-bone à la blue 184
    tenderloin with herbed cheese 164
cherries:
    sour cherry cobbler 273

summer fruit packets 250
cherry cola baked beans 254
cherry pie filling:
    cherry fried pies 276
    cherry pork chops 142
chicken:
    Afghan chicken 109
    apple-honey glazed chicken 109
    apple-raisin stuffed chicken
        thighs 85
    Athenian chicken on the grill 109
    barbecued chicken pizza 40
    barbecued Tex-Mex wings 35
    barbecued wings 16
    Billy's barbecued chicken 102
    Butch's lip-smacking chicken
        drumsticks 112
    chipotle-lime grilled chicken
        thighs 104
    cola can chicken barbecue 103
    easy grilled Cajun chicken 107
    grilled buffalo wings 35
    grilled Cajun chicken 104
    grilled chicken drumsticks 112
    grilled chicken quesadillas 41
    grilled Italian chicken breasts 109
    herbed beer can chicken 82
    honey-citrus chicken 92
    hot Jamaican jerk chicken 99
    hot and sticky grilled thighs with
        apricot glaze 104
    hot and sticky summertime
        chicken 90
    maple barbecued chicken
        drumsticks 112
    marinated barbecued chicken 102
    Mary's barbecued chicken 107
    Moroccan-style smoked chicken 102
    Oriental grilled chicken thighs 104
    Oriental marinated smoked
        chicken 107
    Peruvian grilled chicken 107
    Rasa Malaysian chicken satay 43
    root beer can chicken
        barbecue 103
    simple grilled drumsticks 112
    spicy barbecued chicken 102
    spicy honey-garlic wings 35
    stout beer can chicken
        barbecue 103

sweet California beer can chicken
barbecue 103
teriyaki wings 35
Thai chicken satay skewers 30
whole barbecued chicken 81
chili-rubbed lamb chops 147
chilies:
New Mexico green chili
burgers 183
zesty white bean burgers 229
chipotle country ribs 145
chipotle maple sauce 141
chipotle-chili steak butter 189
chipotle-lime grilled chicken
thighs 104
chives:
sour cream dressing 227
chocolate:
chocolate ice cream 281
German chocolate sheet cake with
chocolate coconut frosting 275
glazed pears with chocolate
sauce 279
grilled s'mores 267
Texas sheet cake with chocolate
frosting 263
chorizo:
El Paso border beans 255
chuckwagon pork butt 144
chuletas de puerco criollas 142
cilantro:
almond-cilantro pesto 188
cinnamon:
cinnamon-grilled sweet
potatoes 222
open-faced cinnamon crisp 277
citrus artichokes 44
citrus salsa 54
citrus-grilled scallops 65
cobblers 259, 273
coconut:
chocolate coconut frosting 275
coffee bean and gourmet peppercorn
crusted steak 190
cola:
cherry cola baked beans 254
cola baked beans 254
cola can chicken barbecue 103
coleslaw see slaw
company-coming t-bones 184

corn:
barbecued corn 235
cabbage and corn slaw 251
Cajun-grilled corn on the cob 250
corn on the cob with spicy lime
butter 250
cumin grilled corn 250
grilled corn Italian-style 250
grilled garlic potatoes with corn 256
grilled wino corn on the cob 250
teriyaki kabobs 227
Cornish game hens:
citrus marinated Cornish hens 105
grilled Cornish game hens 86
grilled Cornish hens with tarragon
and Dijon mustard 105
John's grilled Cornish game
hens 105
Mexican grilled Cornish hens 105
crabmeat:
crab-stuffed jalapeños 45
crab-stuffed mushrooms 34
cream:
sour cream dressing 227
cucumber:
picnic-style potato salad 232
potato salad with cucumber and
dill 231
tomato, cucumber, and lemon
sauce 73
vegetable kabobs 215
cumin grilled corn 250
curried rack of lamb 148
curry pork chops 142

Dates:
bacon-wrapped dates 38
dill:
garlic and dill grilled potatoes 246
mayonnaise and dill salmon 68
potato salad with cucumber and
dill 231
dressings:
balsamic maple dressing 212
creamy tangy dressing 257
sour cream dressing 227
dried fruit fried pies 276
duck:
Asian grilled duck breasts 106
chargrilled duck breasts with

redcurrant glaze 106
grilled duck breast with ginger,
balsamic vinegar, and orange
sauce 106
grilled duck breasts with plum
glaze 106
grilled herbed duck breasts 89

Eggplant:
garlic-butter grilled eggplant 221
grilled eggplant 221
herb and garlic grilled
eggplant 221
honey-garlic grilled eggplant 221
spicy grilled eggplant 203
vegetable kabobs 215
eggs:
American potato salad with
hard-boiled eggs and sweet
pickles 249

Fajitas:
Bichelmeyer's meat market
fajitas 181
Manuel's fajitas 181
West Texas grilled fajitas 181
fluffy nutters 277
frosting:
buttermilk 275
chocolate 275
chocolate coconut 275
cream cheese 275
fruit:
fruit and vegetable kabobs 227
fruits of the forest packets 274
grandma's fried fruit pies 264
summer fruit packets 250
summer fruit packets with
kirsch 274
summer fruit packets with white
wine 274
tropical fruit packets 274
see also bananas, etc

Garlic:
aïoli 71, 167
angel's bruschetta 42
garlic bread 239
garlic butter 73
garlic and dill grilled potatoes 246

garlic-butter grilled eggplant 221
garlic-Dijon leg of lamb 149
garlic-herb butter 12
ginger-garlic barbecued turkey
drumsticks 113
go-go garlic bread 252
gremolata garlic bread 252
grilled garlic potatoes with
corn 256
grilled garlic skirt steak 194
grilled potatoes with roasted
garlic 223
herb and garlic grilled
eggplant 221
honey-garlic grilled eggplant 221
honey-garlic sauce 35, 224
most delicious garlic-cheese
bread 252
mushroom and garlic sauce 182
parsley-garlic bread 252
roasted garlic grilled tomatoes 200
roasted garlic paste 195
Southern grilled garlic
porterhouse 182
zesty garlic-lime quail 110
gin:
grilled steaks with martini twist 185
gingerroot:
ginger, balsamic vinegar, and
orange sauce 106
ginger-garlic barbecued turkey
drumsticks 113
grilled ginger and red wine lamb
chops 147
grilled ginger swordfish 72
peach-ginger turkey cutlets 96
go-go garlic bread 252
goat:
barbecued cabrito 151
barbecued Texas cabrito 138
Cooper's cabrito 151
jerked cabarito 151
jerked cabrito 151
Kansas City cabrito 151
grandma's fried fruit pies 264
Grape-Nut burgers 218
grapefruit:
grilled citrus tuna 61
green beans see beans

Halibut:
  grilled blue cheese halibut 73
  grilled Chinese halibut 73
  grilled halibut with garlic butter 73
  grilled halibut with pineapple 55
  grilled halibut with tomato,
    cucumber, and lemon sauce 73
ham:
  grilled scallops with ham and
    basil 78
  Yukon gold potato salad with
    Tasso 248
herbs:
  beer and herb shrimp 62
  garlic-herb butter 12
  grilled herbed duck breasts 89
  grilled herby lemon salmon 48
  grilled lemon-herb veal chops 195
  herb and garlic grilled
    eggplant 221
  herb-grilled shrimp 77
  herb-grilled tomatoes 220
  herbed beer can chicken 82
  herbed shark steaks 74
  tomato and herb salsa 72
hickory-smoked herb oysters 37
hitching post grilled artichokes 44
hoisin glaze 143
hoisin marinade 69
holiday green beans 253
honey:
  apple-honey glazed chicken 109
  honey deli-style coleslaw 257
  honey glazed rack of lamb 148
  honey glazed shrimp 88
  honey-citrus chicken 92
  honey-garlic grilled eggplant 221
  honey-garlic sauce 35, 224
  honey-grilled potatoes 223
  peaches with blue cheese and
    honey 270
honeysuckle pineapple 278

Ice cream:
  banana ice cream 281
  chocolate ice cream 281
  homemade vanilla ice cream 272
  peach ice cream 281
  strawberry ice cream 281

Jerk barbecued ribs 116
jerked cabarito 151
jicama:
  fruity salsa 100
juniper sugar-cured salmon 68

King of steak butters 189
kiwifruit:
  summer fruit packets 250

Lamb:
  apple-glazed lamb chops 147
  Arizona rack of lamb 148
  Armenian lamb chops 147
  balsamic vinegar and rosemary leg
    of lamb 149
  barbecued lamb ribs 150
  chili-rubbed lamb chops 147
  classic leg of lamb 149
  curried rack of lamb 148
  garlic-Dijon leg of lamb 149
  Greek-flavored leg of lamb 149
  grilled Denver lamb ribs 136
  grilled ginger and red wine lamb
    chops 147
  honey glazed rack of lamb 148
  lamb chops Dijon 131
  lamb ribs provençal 150
  marinated rack of lamb with
    orange marmalade glaze 148
  Ratami's lamb satay 43
  spiced lamb riblets 150
  spicy barbecue Colorado lamb
    ribs 150
  spicy rotisserie leg of lamb 135
  tandoori rack of lamb 132
  ultimate lamb burger 183
lazy daisy sheet cake with buttermilk
  frosting 275
lemons:
  citrus artichokes 44
  citrus-grilled scallops 65
  grilled artichokes with lemon
    yogurt 44
  grilled herby lemon salmon 48
  grilled lemon-herb veal chops 195
  honey-citrus chicken 92
  lemon and basil salmon 68
  sherry and lemon marinade 108

tomato, cucumber, and lemon
  sauce 73
limes:
  fruity salsa 100
  grilled citrus tuna 61
  honey-citrus chicken 92
  lime and basil tilapia 71
  molasses-lime butter 268
  spicy lime butter 250
  spiky lime carne asada 181
  tequila and lime grilled salmon
    steaks 69
  zesty garlic-lime quail 110

Maître d'hôtel butter 189
mango:
  mango jicama slaw 251
  mango strip steak 190
maple syrup:
  balsamic maple dressing 212
  chipotle maple sauce 141
  maple-barbecued chicken
    drumsticks 112
  maple-barbecued salmon 68
margarita shrimp skewers 36
marinades:
  garlic-herb butter 12
  hoisin marinade 69
  marmalade Dijon 69
  rosemary 91
  sherry and lemon 108
marmalade:
  marmalade Dijon marinade 69
  orange marmalade glaze 148
marshmallow cream:
  fluffy nutters 277
marshmallows:
  grilled s'mores 267
mayonnaise:
  aïoli 71, 167
  mayonnaise and dill salmon 68
meatballs:
  barbecued teriyaki meatballs 39
  bbq sweet and spicy meatballs 24
  smoked grape jelly meatballs 39
  smoked Italian meatballs 39
  smoky cocktail meatballs 39
molasses butter 120
molasses-lime butter 268

mushrooms:
  bacon and olive-stuffed
    mushrooms 34
  blue cheese-stuffed mushrooms 34
  Cajun-style portobello
    mushrooms 228
  crab-stuffed mushrooms 34
  Creole-style stuffed
    mushrooms 216
  grilled rib eye steaks with creamed
    mushrooms 193
  grilled stuffed portobello
    mushrooms 228
  mushrooms Napoleon 228
  Paul's grilled mushrooms 226
  portobello mushroom
    sandwich 229
  roasted red pepper-stuffed
    mushrooms 34
  steak and baby portobellos 185
  stuffed Monterey mushrooms 15
  t-bones and wild mushroom
    medley 184
  vegetable kabobs 215
  veggie burgers 229
mustard:
  Dijon sauce 111
  garlic-Dijon leg of lamb 149
  grilled Dijon swordfish steaks 72
  grilled mustard turkey cutlets 111
  hanger steaks with mustard jus 186
  lamb chops Dijon 131
  Lola's mustard slather 124
  marmalade Dijon marinade 69
  mustard tarragon cream sauce 187

Nectarines:
  grilled flank steak with
    nectarines 188

Oats:
  veggie burgers 229
olives:
  anchovy sauce 76
  bacon and olive-stuffed
    mushrooms 34
onions:
  beer and cayenne grilled
    onions 219
  Carolina slaw 251

creamy coleslaw 247
Creole-style stuffed
  mushrooms 216
grilled asparagus with red onion
  and orange 224
grilled lollipop onions 199
grilled potato and onion
  packages 256
grilled red onions 219
grilled t-bones with cowboy grilled
  onions 184
Mexican grilled onions 219
onion and rosemary grilled
  squash 225
pepper sandwich 22
picnic-style potato salad 232
vegetable kabobs 215
veggie burgers 229
Yukon gold potato salad with
  Tasso 248
zesty grilled baby onions 219
zesty white bean burgers 229
oranges:
  citrus artichokes 44
  citrus salsa 54
  grilled asparagus with red onion
    and orange 224
  grilled citrus tuna 61
  honey-citrus chicken 92
oregano grilled squash 225
oysters:
  barbecued oysters with spicy garlic
    butter 37
  grilled bay oysters 37
  grilled oysters San Felipe 20
  grilled oysters in whole shell 37
  hickory-smoked herb oysters 37

Papaya:
  fruity salsa 100
  tropical fruit packets 274
parsley:
  gremolata garlic bread 252
  maître d'hôtel butter (king of steak
    butters) 189
  parsley-garlic bread 252
peach jam:
  peach-ginger turkey cutlets 96
peach pie filling:
  peachy baked beans 254

peaches:
  grilled balsamic-glazed
    peaches 280
  grilled peaches and cream 280
  grilled peaches with raspberry
    purée 280
  peach cobbler 259
  peach ice cream 281
  peach-berry cobbler 273
  peaches with blue cheese and
    honey 270
  summer fruit packets 250
  sweet grilled glazed peaches 280
peanut butter:
  grilled s'mores 267
  peanut sauce 30
pears:
  glazed pears 269
    with brandy syrup 279
    with chocolate sauce 279
    with white wine syrup 279
  Moroccan-style glazed pears 279
pecans:
  crunchy red relish 75
peppercorns:
  coffee bean and gourmet
    peppercorn crusted steak 190
  peppered steak with tarragon 185
  steak au poivre rouge 190
pepperoni:
  grilled pizza 26
peppers:
  andouille-stuffed jalapeños 45
  bacon-wrapped jalapeño
    poppers 33
  bruschetta with roasted peppers 42
  chipotle country ribs 145
  chipotle maple sauce 141
  chipotle-chili steak butter 189
  chipotle-lime grilled chicken
    thighs 104
  country ribs with peach jalapeño
    glaze 145
  crab-stuffed jalapeños 45
  Creole-style stuffed
    mushrooms 216
  fruity salsa 100
  grilled chuck pepper steak 192
  grilled swordfish with roasted red
    pepper 72

grilled vegetable platter with
  balsamic maple dressing 212
jalapeño plum sauce 110
jalapeño potato salad 249
mango jicama slaw 251
pepper sandwich 229
pulled pork-stuffed jalapeños 45
red pepper sauce 224
roasted red pepper-stuffed
  mushrooms 34
scallion-stuffed poppers 45
Southern coleslaw 257
Spanish coleslaw 236
vegetable kabobs 215
veggie burgers 229
pesto:
  almond-cilantro pesto 188
  pesto-walnut butter 189
pies:
  apple fried pies 276
  blueberry fried pies 276
  cherry fried pies 276
  dried fruit fried pies 276
  French apple fried pies 276
  grandma's fried fruit pies 264
pineapple:
  bacon-wrapped pineapple
    chunks 38
  fruity salsa 100
  grilled halibut with pineaple 55
  grilled piña colada 278
  grilled pineapple with molasses-
    lime butter 268
  grilled sweet curried pineapple 278
  honeysuckle pineapple 278
  hot buttered rum pineapple 278
  pineapple-bourbon baked beans 254
  spicy grilled turkey cutlets with
    grilled pineapple rings 111
  tropical fruit packets 274
pinto beans see beans
pizzas:
  barbecued chicken pizza 40
  "bit" pizza appetizer 40
  grilled pizza 26
  halftime pizzas 40
  Italian pizza with goat cheese 40
plums:
  jalapeño plum sauce 110

pork:
  Albuquerque-style pork steaks 143
  bacon-wrapped barbecued pork
    loin 146
  barbecued Polish pork loin 128
  barbecued pork butt 124
  black pepper chops with molasses
    butter 120
  bourbon pork tenderloinns 141
  brat burgers 139
  brown sugar pork butt 144
  Buzz's country ribs 145
  Carolina-country barbecued ribs 140
  char siu Chinese barbecued
    pork 145
  cherry pork chops 142
  chipotle country ribs 145
  chuckwagon pork butt 144
  chuletas de puerco criollas 142
  country ribs with peach jalapeño
    glaze 145
  country-style pork ribs with
    Southern barbecue sauce 127
  elegant barbecued pork loin 146
  finger-lickin' ribs 140
  German-style barbecued pork
    sandwich 119
  gourmet pepper-crusted pork
    loin 146
  grilled curry pork chops 142
  grilled pork steaks adobo 143
  grilled pork steaks with hoisin
    glaze 143
  grilled pulled pork quesadillas 41
  herbed pork burgers 139
  Iowa chops with blue cheese
    sauce 142
  Italian burgers 139
  jerk barbecued ribs 116
  Korean-style pork tenderloins 141
  New Orleans andouille burgers 139
  pork tenderloins with chipotle
    maple sauce 141
  pulled pork-stuffed jalapeños 45
  St Louis pork steaks 123
  S.K.'s Malaysian satay 43
  Southern barbecue pork butt 144
  spice-rubbed ribs 140
  spicy southeast pork butt 144
  tangy grilled pork steaks 143

teriyaki pork burgers 115
Tex-Mex country pork loin 146
Thai tenderloins 141
zesty no-salt herbal ribs 140
porterhouse see beef
potatoes:
    American potato salad with
        hard-boiled eggs and sweet
        pickles 249
    baked potatoes on the grill 256
    blue cheese and walnut potato
        salad 248
    garlic and dill grilled potatoes 246
    grilled garlic potatoes with corn 256
    grilled herbed potatoes 207
    grilled potato and onion
        packages 256
    grilled potatoes with roasted
        garlic 223
    grilled potatoes Tuscan-style 223
    honey-grilled potatoes 223
    jalapeño potato salad 249
    Jamaican potato salad 249
    Louisiana-style potato salad 248
    picnic-style potato salad 232
    potato salad with cucumber and
        dill 231
    roasted potato packages 256
    Scandinavian herbed potatoes 223
    Sicilian potato salad 248
    simple grilled potatoes 223
    Yukon gold potato salad with
        Tasso 248
prawn:
    Thai prawn satay 43
profanity salmon 68
provolone-garlic bread 252

Quail:
    Asian grilled quail 110
    barbecued quail 95
    grilled quail 110
    grilled quail with jalapeño sauce 110
    zesty garlic-lime quail 110
quesadillas:
    grilled chicken quesadillas 41
    grilled pulled pork quesadillas 41
    grilled quesadillas 27
    spicy gourmet grilled quesadillas 41
    steak quesadillas 41

Raisins:
    apple-raisin stuffed chicken
        thighs 85
    cabbage slaw with apple and
        raisins 257
raspberries:
    fruits of the forest packets 274
red snapper:
    grilled red snapper 75
    grilled red snapper with crunchy
        red relish 75
    grilled red snapper with soy sauce
        and avocado 75
    grilled snapper with shallot
        butter 75
    Mexican grilled red snapper 58
relish:
    crunchy red relish 75
Rib Doctor rib eye steaks 193
Romanian beef tenderloin 187
rosemary:
    balsamic vinegar and rosemary leg
        of lamb 149
    blue cheese, rosemary, and balsamic
        vinegar butter 180
    grilled veal chops with
        rosemary 180
    onion and rosemary grilled
        squash 225
    rosemary marinade 91
    scallops grilled on rosemary 78
rubs:
    basic barbecue 12
    Jack's brisket 180
    Kansas City Rib Doctor pork 124
    spicy 153
    spicy Kansas City brisket 180
    Stu Carpenter's brisket 180
    Texas brisket 180
rum:
    grilled piña colada 278
    hot buttered rum pineapple 278

Salads:
    blue cheese and walnut potato 248
    jalapeño potato 249
    Jamaican potato 249
    Louisiana-style potato 248
    picnic-style potato 232
    potato with cucumber and dill 231
    Sicilian potato 248

sweet potato-apple salad 249
Yukon gold potato with Tasso 248
salmon:
    brown sugar-cured salmon 47
    grilled herby lemon salmon 48
    grilled salmon steaks with
        marmalade Dijon marinade 69
    grilled teriyaki salmon steaks 69
    juniper sugar-cured salmon 68
    lemon and basil salmon 68
    maple barbecued salmon 68
    mayonnaise and dill salmon 68
    profanity salmon 68
    salmon steaks with hoisin
        marinade 69
    tequila and lime grilled salmon
        steaks 69
salsa:
    citrus salsa 54
    fruity salsa 100
    tomato and herb salsa 72
sandwiches:
    German style barbecued pork 119
    pepper 229
    portobello mushroom 229
sauces:
    anchovy 76
    blue cheese 142
    buffalo 35
    chipotle maple 141
    ginger, balsamic vinegar, and
        orange 106
    honey-garlic 35, 224
    "hot" barbecue 183
    jalapeño plum 110
    mushroom and garlic 182
    mustard tarragon cream 187
    peanut 30
    red pepper 224
    Southern barbecue 127
    teriyaki 35
    Tex-Mex 35
    tomato barbecue 13
    tomato, cucumber, and lemon 73
    wasabi 76
sausages:
    armadillo eggs 45
    beans and greens 255
    stuffed Monterey mushrooms 15
scallion-stuffed poppers 45

scallops:
    Caribbean scallops 78
    citrus-grilled scallops 65
    grilled scallop kabobs 78
    grilled scallops with ham and
        basil 78
    scallops grilled on rosemary 78
sesame-grilled trout 70
shallots:
    béarnaise butter 168
    bourbon and shallot sauce 182
    hanger steaks with shallots 186
    shallot butter 75
shark:
    anticucho-style grilled shark 74
    Asian-grilled shark steak 74
    grilled shark to die for 57
    herbed shark steaks 74
    marinated grilled shark 74
    sherry and lemon marinade 108
shrimp:
    bacon-wrapped shrimp 38
    beer and herb shrimp 62
    charcoal-grilled shrimp 19
    grilled acadian peppered
        shrimp 77
    grilled shrimp primavera 77
    herb-grilled shrimp 77
    honey grilled shrimp 36
    margarita shrimp skewers 36
    shrimp bruschetta 42
    simple grilled shrimp 77
    spicy grilled shrimp 36
    zesty grilled shrimp 36
slaw:
    cabbage and corn slaw 251
    cabbage slaw with apple and
        raisins 257
    Carolina slaw 251
    coleslaw with creamy tangy
        dressing 257
    creamy coleslaw 247
    honey deli-style coleslaw 257
    mango jicama slaw 251
    Southern coleslaw 257
    Spanish coleslaw 236
    sweet and sassy vanilla slaw 251
Snickers delight dessert tortillas 277

spinach:
  Creole-style stuffed
    mushrooms 216
  grilled tilapia with spinach and
    cherry tomatoes 71
squash:
  grilled patty pan squash 211
  grilled squash 225
  grilled squash parmesan 225
  onion and rosemary grilled
    squash 225
  oregano grilled squash 225
  summertime grilled squash 225
steak see beef
steak au poivre rouge 190
strawberries:
  strawberry ice cream 281
  summer fruit packets 250
summer fruit packets 250
  with kirsch 274
  with white wine 274
summertime grilled squash 225
sweet potatoes:
  cinnamon-grilled sweet
    potatoes 222
  grilled candied sweet potatoes 222
  grilled sweet potato sticks 222
  grilled sweet potatoes 204
  Jamaican grilled sweet potatoes 222
  sweet potato-apple salad 249
swordfish:
  grilled Dijon swordfish steaks 72
  grilled ginger swordfish 72
  grilled swordfish:
    with fresh tomato and herb
      salsa 72
    with roast red pepper 72
  grilled swordfish steaks with citrus
    salsa 54

Tarragon:
  mustard tarragon cream sauce 187
tequila:
  margarita shrimp skewers 36
  tasty tequila tri-tip 197
  tequila and lime grilled salmon
    steaks 69
teriyaki sauce 35

tilapia:
  African tilapia 71
  grilled tilapia 52
  grilled tilapia with spinach and
    cherry tomatoes 71
  lime and basil tilapia 71
  spicy grilled tilapia with aïoli 71
tofu:
  teriyaki tofu and fruit kabobs 227
tomato barbecue sauce 13
tomatoes:
  crunchy red relish 75
  green bean casserole with tomatoes
    and mozzarella 253
  grilled green tomatoes 220
  grilled stuffed portobello
    mushrooms 228
  grilled tilapia with spinach and
    cherry tomatoes 71
  grilled tomato melts 220
  herb-grilled tomatoes 220
  roasted garlic grilled tomatoes 200
  spicy grilled tomatoes 220
  tomato, cucumber, and lemon
    sauce 73
  tomato and herb salsa 72
  tomato-basil bruschetta 29
  vegetable kabobs 215
    with cherry tomatoes 227
tortillas:
  carne asada 154
  fluffy nutters 277
  grilled quesadillas 27
  grilled s'mores 267
  Manuel's fajitas 181
  open-faced cinnamon crisp 277
  open-faced mascarpone gorgozola
    torte 277
  West Texas grilled fajitas 181
trout:
  Cajun-grilled trout with apple
    salsa 70
  grilled spicy trout 70
  grilled trout with Thai sweet
    glaze 70
  "hot" grilled trout 51
  sesame-grilled trout 70
tuna:
  blackened tuna steaks 76
  gourmet pepper-grilled tuna 76

grilled citrus tuna 61
  grilled tuna in anchovy sauce 76
  seared tuna in wasabi sauce 76
turkey:
  drumsticks in sweet and spicy
    barbecue sauce 113
  ginger-garlic barbecued turkey
    drumsticks 113
  grilled buttermilk turkey
    drumsticks 113
  grilled mustard turkey cutlets 111
  grilled turkey drumsticks 113
  grilled turkey scallopini with Dijon
    sauce 111
  grilled turkey tenderloins with
    rosemary marinade 91
  healthy grilled burgers 189
  hoisin-glazed turkey
    tenderloins 108
  Mexican turkey drumsticks 113
  peach-ginger turkey cutlets 96
  plum-glazed Szechwan
    tenderloins 108
  spicy grilled turkey cutlets with
    grilled pineapple rings 111
  tarragon turkey tenderloins 108
  teriyaki turkey cutlets 111
  turkey drumsticks with fruity
    salsa 100
  turkey tenderloins with sherry and
    lemon marinade 108
turnip greens:
  beans and greens 255
turnips:
  beans and greens 255

Veal:
  baron's grilled veal chops 195
  grilled basil veal chops 195
  grilled lemon-herb veal chops 195
  grilled veal chops:
    with roasted garlic paste 195
    with rosemary 177
vegetables:
  fruit and vegetable kabobs 227
  grilled vegetable platter with
    balsamic maple dressing 212
  grilled vegetable platter with fresh
    basil vinaigrette 226

Mediterranean grilled
    vegetables 226
  Tuscan grilled summer
    vegetables 226
  vegetable kabobs 215
  vegetable kabobs with cherry
    tomatoes 227
  see also potatoes, etc
vinaigrette, fresh basil 226
vinegar:
  balsamic hanger steaks 163
  balsamic maple dressing 212
  balsamic vinegar and rosemary leg
    of lamb 149
  blue cheese, rosemary, and balsamic
    vinegar butter 189

Walnuts:
  blue cheese and walnut potato
    salad 248
  pesto-walnut butter 189
wasabi sauce 76
water chestnuts, bacon-wrapped 38
wine:
  glazed pears 269
  glazed pears with white wine
    syrup 279
  grilled wino corn on the cob 250
  red wine short ribs 196
  summer fruit packets with white
    wine 274

Zucchini:
  grilled vegetable platter with
    balsamic maple dressing 212